Other Books by Paul Hellyer

Agenda: A Plan for Action (1971)

Exit Inflation (1981)

Jobs for All: Capitalism on Trial (1984)

Canada at the Crossroads: A Liberal Agenda for the 90's and Beyond (1990)

Damn the Torpedoes: My Fight to Unify Canada's Armed Forces (1990)

Funny Money: A Common Sense Alternative to Mainline Economics (1994)

Surviving the Global Financial Crisis: The Economics of Hope for Generation X (1996)

Arundel Lodge: A Little Bit of Old Muskoka (1996)

The Evil Empire: Globalization's Darker Side (1997)

Stop: Think (1999)

Goodbye Canada (2001)

One Big Party: To Keep Canada Independent (2003)

A Miracle in Waiting: Economics that Make Sense (2010)

Light at the End of the Tunnel: A Survival Plan for the Human Species (2010)

The Money Mafia: A World in Crisis (2014)

Hope Restored: An Autobiography (2018)

LIBERATION !
THE ECONOMICS OF HOPE

PAUL HELLYER

Front Cover Design: Ronnie Pereira.

Published by:
Trine Day LLC
PO Box 577
Walterville, OR 97489
1-800-556-2012
www.TrineDay.com
trineday@icloud.com

Library of Congress Control Number: 2020944671

Hellyer, Paul T.
Liberated! The Economics of Hope—1st ed.
p. cm.

Epub (ISBN-13) 978-1-63424-324-7
Mobi (ISBN-13) 978-1-63424-325-4
Print (ISBN-13) 978-1-63424-323-0
1. International finance. 2. Finance -- Government Policy. 3. Monetary policy --
United States -- History. 4. Global environmental change. 5. Unidentified flying
objects -- Sightings and encounters 6. Human-alien encounters. I. Hellyer, Paul
T. II. Title

FIRST EDITION
10 9 8 7 6 5 4 3 2 1

Distribution to the Trade by:
Independent Publishers Group (IPG)
814 North Franklin Street
Chicago, Illinois 60610
312.337.0747
www.ipgbook.com

For
All children, grandchildren and great-grandchildren who deserve the
right to live, not die.

ACKNOWLEDGMENTS

I have many people to thank for their help with my 16th and final book. First, my thanks to Lucas Kim and my assistant Nina Moskaliuk for helping to type the Manuscript. Usually Nina does most of the work but this time she had to bow out after the first chapter due to the Coronavirus Pandemic.

Mere words are inadequate to express my appreciation to my three readers/editors, Kent Hotaling, Larry Farquharson, and Noel Cooper, for examining the manuscript with their very sharp eyes. The number of additions, deletions and good ideas they presented would require a calculator to record, not to mention typos and spelling errors. I am deeply grateful to each one of them.

My friend, editor and publisher Kris Millegan deserves a bow of appreciation for recognizing the urgency of getting the subject matter of the book into the public domain and for making the miracle happen.

Beatrice Bussiere Shilton earned great praise for producing the drawings in Chapters 1 and 2 under the pressure of great time constraints. Thank you Bea.

My most profound debt is to Sandra's nephew Peter Meades who has been living at our place while waiting for recall to his job. Peter was aware of my desperation and filled the breech. His nimble fingers typed most of the manuscript, and his quick mind was responsible for most of the research. Without Peter, there would be no book!

Last, but certainly not least I want to thank my wife Sandra for her patience and understanding this fourth and final time. She will have another star in her crown in heaven.

TABLE OF CONTENTS

DISCLOSURE

Normally a book begins with a brief introduction, but this one is different. I am 97 years old in August 2020. This is almost certainly my last book. Consequently I feel a moral obligation to share some of the information that I have discovered beginning in 2005 that I have labelled "The Broader Reality." I warn you that some of it sounds stranger than Science Fiction but I can assure you that to the best of my knowledge every word is the truth.

Until early in the 21st century I was unaware that we Earthlings were not alone. It is true that when I was Minister of National Defence for Canada I received UFO sighting reports. I was too busy unifying the Canadian Navy, Army, and Air Force into a Canadian Defence Force that I didn't pay much attention to them. About 80% of the sightings could be explained as natural phenomena with the balance being "Unidentified Flying Objects" in the literal sense, hence UFOs.

In 2003 a young bilingual chap from Ottawa, Pierre Juneau, began sending me information about UFOs that I told him I was too busy to read. He was very patient and suggested that I just put it on a shelf for a rainy day. He urged me to watch an ABC special by Peter Jennings that included testimony by retired USAF pilots, commercial airline pilots, air traffic controllers, police officers and others who all claimed that they had seen UFOs. I couldn't fathom any reason why they would go on air and say that they had seen one or more UFOs if it were not the truth.

It was a book that Pierre sent me which finally convinced me. It was entitled *The Day After Roswell,*[1] by Lt. Col. Philip Corso, a retired U.S. Army Intelligence officer. It looked intriguing but it wasn't until the summer of 2005 when I got around to reading it. I realized it was real, and had that fact confirmed by a retired USAF general who said every word is true and more. The "more" included the fact that there had been face to face meeting between U.S. officials and visitors from other star systems.

I decided to accept an outstanding invitation to speak at a symposium Victor Viggiani and Mike Bird were holding at Convocation Hall at the University of Toronto on September 25th because I thought that U.S. taxpayers and, indeed, everyone in the world had the right to know what was going on because the stakes were so high. I was the last speaker after Stanton Friedman, Richard Dolan and Stephen Bassett, all distinguished ufologists. Following a few preliminary remarks, I said, "UFOs are as real as the airplanes flying overhead".

This gave me the dubious distinction of being the first person of cabinet rank in what was then the G8 group of countries to state categorically, without any reservations that UFOs are real. I had promised my fiancé, Sandra Bussiere, the widow of my best friend ever who had agreed to marry me one week later on October 1, 2005, that the speech would be a "one off" affair. I couldn't possibly have been more wrong. Documents both classified and unclassified arrived from several jurisdictions, dozens of books came in the mail and I eventually read every one of them. Experts wanted to brief me and I soon found myself launched on a new career of examination and discourse which would change my life forever and obligate me to share my seemingly incredible conclusions.

I am putting in two facts to give you a glimpse of the Broader Reality.

On February 2, 1961, an armada of about 50 UFOs flew south from Russia and then turned around and headed for the North Pole just in time to avoid the panic button being pushed by the headquarters of the Supreme Headquarters of the Allied Powers in Europe (SHAPE) which might have triggered another world war. Once the crisis was recognized as a false alarm, SHAPE ordered an investigation into the UFO phenomenon that was titled *An Assessment: An Evaluation of a Possible Military Threat to Allied Forces in Europe*, and written over a three-year period from 1961-1964. The conclusions of the study were earth-shattering. The authors determined, with absolute certainty, that we have been actively visited by representatives of at least four extraterrestrial civilizations for thousands of years.

It was a near miracle that the public learned of the existence of *An Assessment*. Our benefactor is retired Army Command Sergeant Major, a decorated Korean War veteran, who was given what we call a "plum assignment" at SHAPE (Supreme Headquarters Allied Powers in Europe) just outside of Paris where he worked as an intelligence analyst and was given a Cosmic Top Secret clearance, the highest in the Command. It was there that his profound inner transformation from innocent "good soldier" to disillusioned, concerned citizen took place.

His story, as he tells it, is as follows. Late one night when he was working the graveyard shift, he was bored to distraction. The colonel in charge thought he would enjoy shocking Dean by giving him a Cosmic Top Secret document to read. It was *An Assessment.* "By the time Dean finished reading that book, the old, highly structured, and predictable world he had taken for granted all his life was in shambles all around him as he contemplated an entirely new, incredible reality."[2]

People often quote me as saying that there are just four species after hearing this story. In reality, there are many more. U.S. Army Sergeant Clifford Stone, who worked in a unit that retrieved crashed UFOs said the manual he had been given in association with his work listed 54 species and how they should be handled.[3] If you think of the billions of star systems that exist in the cosmos it is likely that there are thousands and perhaps millions of species.

THE FIVE PLAGUES

The sum of what I have learned about the "broader reality" would take several books. The most urgent conclusions can be summed up in the following five plagues.

It may have been the Coronavirus Pandemic that made me think of that word. In any event it triggered my memory of the story in the Jewish and Christian Bibles of the Exodus of the Children of Israel from Egypt. They had long been slaves of the Pharaoh who exploited them for his own benefit. The Creator asked Moses to lead the Israelites to freedom but that was easier said than done. A total of 10 plagues were required the 10th and final was the Passover during which the first-born of everyone, both man and beast, was killed except for the Israelites who had been instructed to put the blood of a lamb on the lintels of their doors. They would be saved and allowed to leave for the land promised to them by their father Abraham. They were passed over.[4]

Now the tables have turned. There are five plagues but not necessarily less lethal, and we have brought them on ourselves.

PLAGUE NO. 1: THE FOURTH REICH

I began to write this section three days after the 75th anniversary of V/E Day. I saw the Premier of Ontario standing at attention in the centre of a very small group of servicemen and women who were saluting the flag. Queen Elizabeth II said a few words reminding us of that great victory 75 years ago. I was in uniform there, and for most of my life I have learned the truth. We didn't win! We lost! May 12, 1945 should be re-designated as DDIE, the day of deception in Europe.

As early as October 1940, years before Germany surrendered, the Council on Foreign Relations headquartered in New York City, decided Germany would lose and that it should plan for an even greater Empire comprising the United Kingdom, the Western Hemisphere, and the Far East.[5] But the CFR were not the only ones who knew, after the U.S.S.R. and the United States entered the war in support of the Allies, that Hitler would lose. So they began to make plans accordingly. They began to move large sums of money out of Germany to hide in places where they would have access to it.

Then, long before World War II was over, the Nazis began to build a base in Antarctica. They sent many of their best scientists and engineers with all the necessary support staff to establish a fully-equipped government-in-exile. It was called the New Berlin.

The American government was fully aware of the development so Defense Secretary George C. Marshall dispatched the equivalent of a naval armada to attack and destroy this residual threat. The operation organized by Rear Admiral Richard E. Byrd Jr., USN (Ret.), officially known as Task Force 68, comprised 4700 men, 13 ships including one carrier, and 33 aircraft.[6]

The flotilla refuelled in Argentina and then proceeded to Antarctica where it was expected to achieve its mission quickly. Instead, it was forced to retreat when it was repelled by flying discs that could have been either German or Reptilian, the one ET species that has been regarded as hostile, including its collaboration with the Nazis before and during World War II.[7] The discs destroyed an American ship and killed 68 mean in a brief engagement that forced Byrd to retreat and terminate the operations.[8] (The Wikipedia report of the reason for the task force is a complete fabrication).

Admiral Byrd was so angry that he suggested using nuclear weapons to eliminate the enemy base. By the winter of 1947, however, the Nazi influence on American policy was such that nothing was done. That influence was largely due to an earlier project known as "Operation Paperclip" which brought hundreds of Nazi scientists and technicians to the U.S. where they were given American citizenship, new names and credentials, and then appointed to important jobs in both civil and military establishments.

It's true that President Harry S. Truman, who had approved the operation, had decreed that no one who had been active in the Nazi party would be eligible but that condition was almost totally ignored. Many more Nazi specialists were hired by the military-industrial complex and when Allen Dulles finally became Director of the Central Intelligence Agency (CIA) he, with the support of his brother John Foster Dulles, managed to bring an additional wave of Nazi immigrants who, in concert with those who had come before them, managed to infiltrate many branches of the U.S. establishment.

Emboldened by their success, the Nazis concluded that a Fourth Reich was a real possibility. So even though the United States had no significant enemies at that time the plotters embarked on the greatest building of military power in the history of humankind. This strategy, as we learned later from my good friend Carol Rosin, was simple. It was given to her by her boss Werner von Braun, the world famous missile expert. He had been an active Nazi but mellowed in his senior years and briefed Rosin who worked for him.[9]

To justify huge military expenditures you have to have an enemy. So, first it would be the communists, then it would be the terrorists, and finally it would be the extraterrestrials. That was the way to justify a policy of continuous war, and that is exactly the way it has played out. The word communism is anathema to Americans so it didn't take much effort to create hate of the Soviets. When the Berlin Wall came down, however, and Russia was open for U.S. capital investment, a quick shift to the terrorists became urgent.

There weren't enough terrorists to justify the wars that the Pentagon had planned for the Middle East but, for some reason, the Israeli Prime Minister and his Mossad Intelligence organization dreamed up the idea of an attack on the World Trade Centre in New York City, another Pearl Harbour, as it was referred to in an early draft of the Pentagon Plans for a new American Century.[10] In any event this terrible tragedy had the desired effect and prepared the American electorate for the attack on Iraq, even though there was absolutely no hint of involvement by that country in one of the greatest mass murders of modern times. Incidentally, I have since been allowed to read a 350-page book outlining the extent of the Israeli involvement in both the planning of the attack and the subsequent cover up.

That book is not available to the general public but I would strongly urge you to read *Where Did the Towers Go? Evidence of Directed Free Energy Technology on 9/11*, by Dr. Judy Wood. Judy won't say who did it but has almost 500 pages of meticulous evidence she will convince you that the official version was fiction.

The whole episode, including the attack on Iraq, changed the world forever. We had to endure frustrating and time-consuming clearance to board an aircraft. President George W. Bush invoked the support of NATO countries in the war against the alleged terrorist attacks.[11] Many civil rights were taken away. Sadly Christianity was given a bad name and the rapport that had existed between religions for centuries evaporated overnight.

The Pentagon had been given a license to inevitable wars in the Middle East, as was its plan. It was also able to convince a naïve Congress to increase the defense budget by 100% in one year, an incredible achievement from its point of view. An unseen negative was the reaction of China and Russia who were well aware that something was happening and that they should join the race.

If it wasn't obvious before it was recognized by a few that the government of the U.S. had shifted from the President and Congress to a group that I and others have labelled the Cabal. It is an informal group comprised of the Illuminati, the "Three Sisters" officially known as the Bilderberg Group, The Council on Foreign Relations and the Trilateral Commission, some of whose members are the Banking Cartel, at the apex, the Oil Cartel, the Trans National Corporations, the intelligence groups including the CIA, the FBI, the NSA, the Israeli Mossad and the British MI6, plus a huge swath of the U.S. military, especially the Air Force and Navy, and now the new Space Force. They have also been referred to from time to time as the "shadow government" or "the alternate government."

This is the power that the late U.S. Senator Inouye, of Hawaii, referred to "with its own Air Force, its own Navy, its own fundraising mechanism, and the ability to pursue its own ideas of the national interest, and free from all checks and balances, and free from the law itself."[12]

The Cabal is the same group that President Bill Clinton was referring to when senior White House press correspondent Sarah McClendon asked him why he didn't reveal more about the ET phenomenon. His reply: "Sarah there is a government within the government, and I don't control it."[13]

That was the truth, and it gives me the shivers to know that the President of the United States, the most powerful military country on Earth, and Commander-in-Chief of its Armed Forces, is unaware of the projects and plans of the troops he theoretically commands.

It has been that way for a long time. When scientists moved the airship that had been recovered from a crash near Roswell New Mexico in July 1947 from its temporary location to an underground facility in Nevada, known as Area 51, President Dwight Eisenhower wanted to know what they were doing there. They refused to tell him. It was only when he threatened to send in the Army that they agreed to let him have 3 or 4 friends from the CIA take a look around. They found that the scientists were back engineering the crashed vehicle. Other presidents have received similar treatment.

Dr. Michael Wolfe, who had a security clearance higher than any president, explained that the underground base at Area 51 is a sprawling city the size of Rhode Island that has continued to grow, with a sister base called S4 some 12 miles away, and another named Indian Springs.[14] Only President Obama has been allowed to land at Nellis Air Force Base, and to the best of our knowledge no American President has been allowed to visit or inspect the vast installations in the area.

In the same radio interview with Chris Stoner before Wolfe died in September 2000, he said that President George H. W. Bush had been the most knowledgeable of all the presidents, probably because he had been head of the CIA. This is the same President Bush who announced the advent of the New World Order. It sounded like a new era of peace, harmony, and love. But that is not the case. It is to be an unelected totalitarian world government of, by and for the rich elite. The word 'fascist' sounds less offensive than a Fourth Reich.

For those who are not familiar with the depth of the infiltration a few words from the cover of a book titled *America's Nazi Secret,* by John Loftus, a former U.S. government prosecutor and former Army officer may be helpful.

> "The Nuremburg trials were fixed. The US Justice Department did it. Some of America's most influential families funded Hitler. Ambitious lawyers in Washington covered it up under a cloak of national security. The Justice Department brought Nazis into America by the thousands to be trained as cold war spies."
>
> "The Attorney General personally sponsored some of the worst war criminals for immigration to the USA, including the chief of the Ukrainian security service, Mykola Lebed. His troops murdered tens of thousands of Poles, Ukrainians, and Jews, including Simon Wiesenthal's mother."
>
> "In 1985, the Justice Department pawned this Ukrainian mass murderer off to Congress as an innocent leader of the Anti-Nazi resistance. Almost everything the Justice Department has ever told Congress about Nazis in America has been a conscious and deliberate lie. The hunt for Nazi war criminals has been a mere public relations effort to placate Jews and WWII veterans."[15]

It seems self-apparent that in the early post-World War II years America sold its soul in exchange for space technology, including killing machines previously unheard of except in science fiction. Tragically, the future of the human species, as well as our relationship with our diverse extraterrestrial neighbours, seems to be at play on the cosmic chessboard.

Until now I haven't mentioned names although now I think the time has come to do so. The one exception has been David Rockefeller who ably stated the end game in his *Memoirs*.

> "Some even believe we are a part of a secret Cabal working against the best interests of the United States, characterizing my family and me as 'internationalists' and of conspiring with others around the world to build a more integrated global political and economic structure, one world, if you will. If that's the charge, I stand guilty, and I am proud of it."[16]

I would respectfully disagree! The 60-year dash down the road to rule by "bankers and elite" has not produced a better world. On the contrary! It has created a world of increasing misery, uncertainty and hopelessness. After World War II many patriots swore "never again." Yet the tell-tale ingredients seem to be re-appearing before our very eyes. When it comes to the life and death issues we humans are slow learners, and tend to repeat our worst mistakes. So what do we need?

We need a full stop of just about every policy trend initiated by the New World Order (NWO) since the 1960's. First, then, a "full stop" to facilitate a 180-degree U turn. As we used to say in the army, "about ta".

Then a joint Congressional Committee should be established to seek the truth from the hundreds of potential whistleblowers anxious to tell the truth of what they have seen. It would be necessary to grant an amnesty under the National Security Act, so witnesses could testify without fear of winding up in jail.

None of these huge issues are partisan issues. They are people issues related to whether or not we will live or die. As the truth is told each Congressman and Congresswoman will be faced with the choice of being a peacemaker or a warmonger.

PLAGUE NO. 2: GLOBAL WARMING

The Cabal that I mentioned is the proactive creator of all of the plagues except one. In the case of Global Warming it is passive creator. They pretend that there is no problem and spend tens of millions of dollars creating fake news to that effect.

In the last 15 years I have spoken to American audiences innumerable times. I get a warm reception. But all too often I get an email from one of my American cousins saying something along the following lines: "Hellyer (or Paul) I agree with every single word you said except for that nonsense about global warming. That is just a hoax. What we see is just a natural cycle. So you should check your facts on that one."

My response is always: "Sorry, I have checked the facts and I couldn't disagree more!"

The scientist who had the greatest impact on my knowledge and understanding of the issue is Dr. James E. Hansen, a member of the National Academy of Sciences, an adjunct professor in the Department of Earth and Environmental Sciences at Columbia University and at Columbia's Earth Institute, and director of the NASA Goddard Institute for Space Studies. My wife Sandra and I were listening to him being interviewed on the radio a few years ago and found him to be both interesting and convincing. Sandra bought one of his books, *Storms of my Grandchildren*[17] and gave it to me for my birthday.

It was not a light read because it was pure science. But it was compelling for me because he raised and dealt with all alternative reasons for global warming, such as it being a natural cycle, and firmly established the fact that we Earthlings <u>are</u> responsible for the phenomenon and that it is within our power to do something about it. It is a brave stand that has resulted in censure and attracted criticism from the naysayers, who have their own agenda. That is the high price paid by pioneers.

On the other hand, many admire Hansen. I agree with the following plug from Bill McKibben, coordinator of 350.org and author of *The End of Nature*:

> Jim Hansen is the planet's great hero. He offered us the warning we needed twenty years ago, and has worked with enormous courage ever since to try and make sure we heeded it. We'll know before long if that effort bears fruit – if it does, literally no one deserves more credit than Dr. Hansen.

Bravo! But I am astonished to learn that the warning came twenty years ago and that so little action has resulted. Is there no one capable of reading the tea leaves when the evidence is so obvious to anyone keeping records of rising temperatures? It is also obvious that the storms Dr. Hansen predicted for his grandchildren are already happening, all over the world! So many have been reported from one country after another, and the consequences have been so horrendous, that I started to keep a file on them for the first time in my long life. Hundreds of people have been drowned, and thousands have lost everything they own.

More solid evidence of the widespread nature of global warming came like a lightning strike to anyone who could read when they opened the Toronto *Globe and Mail* newspaper on July 29, 2010. The headline read SIGNS OF WARMING EARTH "UNMISTAKABLE." Each of the past three decades has been the hottest on record, according to a new report that offers stunning evidence for climate change. The study was the most extensive ever done on global warming. The information is 10 years out of date but would be more dramatic now!

Indeed the facts assembled by the U.S. National Oceanic and Atmospheric Administration (NOAA) in a report co-edited by researchers in the United States, Canada, Britain and Australia, based on data from 10 climate indicators measured by 160 research groups in 48 countries, are ominous.

SEA LEVEL RISING

For the past 15 years, sea levels have been rising a little more than one-eighth of an inch per year.

SNOW COVER DECLINING

Snow cover in the Arctic showed a continuation of relatively shorter snow seasons.

AIR TEMPERATURES RISING

Average surface temperatures in the last three decades have been progressively warmer than all earlier decades.

OCEAN TEMPERATURE RISING

Warming has been noted as far as 6,000 feet below the surface but most of the heat is accumulating in the oceans' near-surface layers.

SEA ICE DECLINING

The summer sea ice cover was the third-lowest recorded since 1979.

HUMIDITY RISING

Humidity from the tropical Pacific contributed to unusually low temperatures in northern and central Mexico as the humid air mixed with cold fronts.

SEA AIR TEMPERATURE RISING

A warmer climate means higher sea levels, humidity and temperatures in the air and ocean.

GLACIERS DECLINING

Early data shows that 2009 will likely be the 19th consecutive year glaciers have lost mass.

OCEAN HEAT RISING

Studies show oceans absorb most of the extra heat added from the build-up of heat-trapping gases.

LAND AIR TEMPERATURES RISING

The surface air temperature record is compiled from weather stations around the world. Analyses show an upward trend across the globe.

While the facts speak loud and clear they are all the more dramatic when presented in graph form in bright red ink!

One of the most dramatic illustrations I have seen was a full double-page spread in the Toronto *Globe and Mail* in its weekend paper of Saturday, March 16, 2013. Folio:

Climate Science. Title: "The incredible shrinking summer ice cover."

This was followed by schematic illustrations of the Arctic ice cover in 1982, 2002, and 2012.

For 1982, the icecap extended from one side of the double page to the other – 7.5 million square km.

In 2002, the icecap extended about three quarters of the way representing 5.36 million square km.

In 2012, the icecap extended just under halfway - 3.41 million square km.

The bottom line on the page reads: "Scientists now say the Arctic will become ice free during the summer sometime between 2015 and 2030. The year 2030 = 0."

Does anyone understand what this means? Fire!!! Our planetary home is on fire and no one has even bothered to call the fire brigade. The apathy is enough to make one's blood boil. Recent articles I have read draw attention to the food chain, beginning with the oceans.

There will not be enough small fish in Antarctica and the North Atlantic to keep the chain alive. Rising temperatures will reduce the amount of arable land and create food shortages. Rising sea levels will displace millions more people when we already have the most displaced persons ever, yet the leaders of the Group of Twenty nations, like Emperor Nero of Rome before them, are content to play their fiddles while the planet burns. To continue the analogy, by the time they wake up, there will be nothing left but the ashes.

My country, Canada, is one of the worst. Thousands of young people with foresight have been parading because they sense the pending disaster. Our government pledges to do something quite inadequate by 2050. By then the game will be over, and lost. Some of us will remember that when it came to the crunch only the Aboriginal Lifetime Elders stood up for our grandchildren and great grandchildren. What has been a problem will be a plague that will make the Coronavirus Pandemic look like a blip on the radar.

There is a cure, although someone will have to take the lead and shame the Cabal into positive action. Dr. Michael Wolfe told us years ago that the U.S. Armed Forces had developed zero point energy decades ago.[18] That is the energy that exists everywhere in the universe and has to replace oil and gas as it replaced wood and coal.

The substitutions has to be pursued with the urgency of a war because that is what it is – a war for survival. I have long argued that what we have to do is the obverse of what was done in World War II. Then, all of the automobile, refrigeration and washing machine manufacturers were converted in to the production of armaments. Now we have to convert the armament plants into the production of zero point energy motors and heaters and put them in every truck, car, tractor, boat, airplane and house in the world. The number of jobs created would be enormous and the benefit from arresting global warming would be incalculable.

In the end the Cabal will have to be engaged. But now, immediately, some small country will have to show the way. It is still possible that one of the worst plagues in history, for which there is no vaccine, can be avoided.

PLAGUE NO. 3: GEO-ENGINEERING, CHEMTRAILS, HAARP, & THE IONIZED SKY

By sheer coincidence the day I began to write this section was the first sunny day in quite a while with its beautiful blue sky. Mid-morning I looked out and behold two horizon to horizon chemtrails just starting to open up and cover a section of the sky with its unique tell-tale cloud. They didn't have the decency to stop their poisonous routine during the Coronavirus Pandemic. I hate to see the sky go gray but it's the composition of the emulsion that concerns me most.

My concern is shared by neuro-surgeon Dr. Russell Blaylock who reveals some shocking firsts that I would like to share verbatim.

> The Internet is littered with stories of "chemtrails" and geo-engineering to combat 'global warming' and until recently I took these stories

with a grain of salt. One of the main reasons for my skepticism was that I rarely saw what they were describing in the skies. But over the past several years I have noticed a great number of these trails and I have to admit they are not like the contrails I grew up seeing in the skies. They are extensive, quite broad, are laid in a definite pattern and slowly evolve into artificial clouds. Of particular concern is that there are now so many dozens every day that they are littering the skies.

My major concern is that there is evidence that they are spraying tons of nanosized aluminum compounds. It has been demonstrated in the scientific and medical literature that nanosized particles are infinitely more reactive and induce intense inflammation in a number of tissues. Of special concern is the effect of these nanoparticles on the brain and spinal cord, as a growing list of neurodegenerative diseases, including Alzheimer's dementia, Parkinson's disease and Lou Gehrig's disease (ALS) are strongly related to exposure to environmental aluminum.

Nanoparticles of aluminum are not only infinitely more inflammatory, they also easily penetrate the brain by a number of routes, including the blood and olfactory nerves (the small nerves in the nose). Studies have shown that these particles pass along the olfactory neural tracts, which connect directly to the area of the brain that is not only most affected by Alzheimer's disease, but also the earliest affected in the course of the disease. It also has the highest level of brain aluminum in Alzheimer's cases.

The intranasal route of exposure makes spraying of massive amounts of nanoaluminum into the skies especially hazardous, as it will be inhaled by people of all ages, including babies and small children for many hours. We know that older people have the greatest reaction to this airborne aluminum. Because of the nanosizing of the aluminum particles being used, home filtering systems will not remove the aluminum, thus prolonging the exposure, even indoors.

In addition to inhaling nanoaluminum, such spraying will saturate the ground, water and vegetation with high levels of aluminum. Normally, aluminum is poorly absorbed from the GI tract, but nanoaluminum is absorbed in much higher amounts. This absorbed aluminum has been shown to be distributed to a number of organs and tissues including the brain and spinal cord. Inhaling this environmentally suspended nanoaluminum will also produce tremendous inflammatory reaction within the lungs, which will pose a significant hazard to children and adults with asthma and pulmonary diseases.

I pray that the pilots who are spraying this dangerous substance fully understand that they are destroying the life and health of their families as well. This is also true of our political officials. Once the soil, plants and water sources are heavily contaminated there will be no way to reverse the damage that has been done.

Steps need to be taken now to prevent an impending health disaster of enormous proportions if this project is not stopped immediately. Otherwise we will see an explosive increase in neurodegenerative diseases occurring in adults and the elderly in unprecedented rates as well as neurodevelopmental disorders in our children. We are already seeing a dramatic increase in these neurological disorders and it is occurring in younger people that ever before.[19]

I brought this problem to the attention of Canadian Prime Minister Justin Trudeau but he has done nothing to rescue his children and ours.

Dane Wigington, GeoengineeringWatch.org is one of the world's most knowledgeable experts on this subject. Here is a quote from his amazing booklet: *Geoengineering: A Chronicle Of Indictment.* I quote:

How many of us have ever known truly natural weather? Global climate intervention/geoengineering/solar radiation management programs are not just an outlandish and unrealistic 'proposal', climate intervention operations have been deployed and steadily expanded for over 70 years with catastrophic consequences. In addition to the stated purpose of 'mitigating' global warming (which all available data confirms geoengineering is making worse overall, not better), there are many additional objectives being carried out in our skies under the guise of geoengineering. The electrically conductive heavy metal particles (that are being sprayed) help to enhance over-the-horizon radar, radio frequency transmissions, and EMP (electromagnetic pulse) offense and defense weaponry. The military industrial complex, of course, never considers the immense consequences of their atmospheric activities and experiments.[20]

Dane suggests, most of us haven't a clue what has been going on. The military have the capability to make it snow in summer or rain in winter. Or they can create an earthquake that only a few experts can recognize as man-made. These are all weapons that can be used in peace or war to punish objectors or enemies, as the case may be.

Covert global climate engineering programs are the single most environmentally destructive assault the human race has ever unleashed against nature and the entire web of life. The list of catastrophic environmental and human health consequences directly connected to the ongoing climate engineering insanity makes these programs mathematically the greatest and most immediate threat we collectively face short of nuclear cataclysm. Climate scientists claim that 'solar radiation management' is the final option for cooling down our rapidly warming world, but is that the truth? Are 'climate intervention' programs actually mitigating the unfolding planetary meltdown? Or further fuelling it overall? How can we expose and halt the global geoengineering omnicide before it is too late?[21]

I agree with Dane's conclusion, which has been confirmed by a retired United States air force general of my acquaintance. But it was my audiologist, Carol Boychuk, who first clued me into the picture, giving me half a dozen of her photographs of chemtrails above our City of Toronto, including one right over the world famous Hospital for Sick Children.

She asked me to get a copy of Elana Freeland's book *Chemtrails, HAARP, and the Full Spectrum Dominance of Planet Earth,* which I read with a combination of acute interest and horror. When I finished, my fury knew no bounds. It is a "must read" for anyone concerned with the survival of the human species!

I thought long and hard before including this final warning. It has been well established that the Coronavirus was developed by the U.S. in cooperation with the Chinese.[21]

We have already been warned that the next virus could be more lethal. Without questioning the authenticity of that statement it is fair to assume that the people who developed the CoViD-19 are working on something much worse. Chemtrails could be used as a more effective means of distribution. The nozzles were developed during the Vietnam War to defoliate the forests. It would be easy to add a virus in the emulsion and infect tens of millions of people in 24 hours. Heaven can only help us if we fail to dismantle the whole chemtrail, HAARP and Ionized sky apparatus at once!

PLAGUE NO. 4: The Electro-Magnetic Fields

This is one I should have been aware of but never gave it a thought. In my youth I was told that Fromm Brothers who ran a successful farm breeding silver foxes for the pelts, growing ginseng and later breeding mink for fur coats had a serious problem when a hydro line was built on their property. I also thought as I drive by the huge hydro towers and their multiple lines of wires that people living too close would have problems, but it was just a passing thought.

Last winter, 2020, a friend put me in touch with Captain Jerry G. Flynn, retired Electronic Warfare Specialist and suggested I get a copy of his book *Hidden Danger, how governments, telecom and electric power utilities suppress the truth about the known hazards of electro-magnetic fields (EMF) radiation*. So I bought the book, took it with me on holiday, and read it from cover to cover. I was fascinated and horrified.

Some of the highlights on the book cover read as follows.

> "Clear evidence was found that radiation from cell phone towers and cell phones CAUSE cancer (in two 2018 studies: the 10-year, $25-million U.S. National Toxicology Project study by the National Institute of Environmental Health Sciences, and an independent 2018 study by the renowned Ramazzini Institute in Italy).
>
> In 2019, Poland's Prime Minister signed the Global Appeal to *Ban 5G on Earth and in Space*.
>
> Class action lawsuits are underway to *stop the rollout of 5G* in Quebec, California and elsewhere around the world (although the news media is complicit and won't tell you).
>
> Scientists say that unless 5G is stopped, humanity won't have to worry about climate change."

Two paragraphs from Jerry's biography tell the story.

> "On leaving the Forces, in my second career, which also lasted 26 years, I was extremely fortunate to have a client list that eventually included the Saudi Arabian government plus other large multinational corporations who collectively had major operations and/or projects in various countries on five continents. Consequently, I quickly embraced all things wireless: a Blackberry cell phone, Wi-Fi routers (in the office and at home); cordless phones (both locations), microwave ovens (both locations), laptop computer (wireless, of course), Bluetooth cell phone and heated seats in my vehicles, electric in-floor radiant heat in my homes, not to mention the silent and invisible EMF (electric field and magnetic field) radiation I was exposed to in my working and living environments.
>
> "In the fall of 2016, cancer very nearly took my life! Out-of-the-blue, I was suddenly stricken with a particularly virulent form of non-Hodgkin lymphoma – which, in hindsight, I attribute solely to my own indefensible stupidity and naiveté in presuming Health Canada had tested and verified that all wireless electronic products on the market were 'safe' for the public to use! My weight quickly dropped from about 175 lbs to less than 130 lbs, and I required an oxygen ma-

chine to breathe day and night! In retrospect, were it not for an excellent medical team and for my beloved wife's tireless attention and endless nursing and for her stubborn determination not to let me go, I would not be here to fight this, what has become, the Mother of all Crimes – which now, unbelievably, threatens all life on earth!"[22]

I, Paul, became so concerned that I removed the Wi-Fi router from our bedroom, asked my wife Sandra to hold the phone two inches from her head, and, not hold her laptop when in her lap when she is checking her email in the morning.

The military application is even more worrisome.

Microwave Radiation, The Military's Perfect Weapon – Emitted by Cell Phone Towers?

All cell phone towers emit <u>non-</u>thermal pulsed microwave radiation – and do so day and night, year-in and year-out! Major militaries, such as those of the USA, of the UK, of Russia, of China and others use – and have used, for decades, – <u>non</u>-thermal pulsed microwave radiation in their invisible, silent, odourless and tasteless weapons to disperse crowds, to disorient, immobilize, harm, injure and kill people. This is why militaries consider microwave radiation to be the "perfect" weapon; it leaves no trace![23]

The plans of the U.S. Military's favourite pawn Elon Musk are indescribably worrisome.

The following was copied from yesterday's (Mar. 22/20) Citizensforsaftech.ca who, thanks to their Director Sharon Noble, issues a daily 'update'.

> "1) The US FCC is using the pandemic as an excuse for this major expansion of the 5G network to ensure that every inch on earth receives signals from which the network can gather data. According to Dafna Tachover (https://wearetheevidence.org/) the million ground stations will transmit using 14-14.5 GHz frequencies and will receive at 10.7-12.7 GHz. These are frequencies that currently are not in use for any devices used by the public and, just like RF signals have never been shown to be safe."[24]

FCC approves SpaceX to deploy up to 1 million small antennas for Starlink internet network.

"The Federal Communications Commission (FCC) has authorized SpaceX to begin rolling out as many as 1 million of the ground antennae the company will need to connect users to its Starlink satellite internet network. Starlink is SpaceX's plan to build an interconnected network, or 'constellation,' of about 12,000 small satellites, to provide high-speed internet to anywhere in the world. The company has launched 360 Starlink satellites in the past year."[25]

Elon Musk has applied to the FCC for permission to launch an additional 30,000 satellites, which, if approved, would give him something like 42,000 satellites? I wonder which international body gave the U.S. and the FCC the right to authorize cluttering up space indescribably?

PLAGUE NO. 5: THE MONEY CREATION MONOPOLY

This one has been chronic and ongoing for hundreds of years. There was a time when monarchs or governments created all the money. Later, there was a period when the money creation function was shared between governments and private bankers. It was called the partial reserve system of banking, when privately owned banks had to have some government created money as reserve against their deposits.

Finally the cunning and very powerful bankers persuaded governments to eliminate the need for cash reserves altogether.

Governments lost their benefit from seigniorage and were in the unhappy position of not having enough money for education, health care, new roads and bridges and all the other needs of the people. Governments could only raise money for essential services by taxation or by borrowing it from the banks and going deeper and deeper into debt in a system of dead end economics.

Meanwhile a group of the most powerful banks, that are sometimes called banksters, have accumulated fortunes in the hundreds of trillions of dollars. It is time to end the grand larceny and restore a balance of power that gives back to the people a fair share of what is justly their own money.

This is what this book is primarily about. People should be liberated from their slavery to debt!!! A significant amount of the material has been borrowed from my earlier books.

CHAPTER ONE

A Little History of Money

*The century on which we are entering can be
and must be the century of the common person.*

–Henry Wallace

My name is Paul Hellyer, a former defense minister
of Canada. And you must be Alice and Roger.
Welcome to our advanced course on money and
banking.

In the course of writing an earlier book I asked scores of friends who are well versed in the subject – if they knew where money comes from. The sample included people with BAs, MAs, PhDs, DDs, BScs, and lots of ordinary 'folk' with vast experience and much common sense. Not one of them had what I would call a working knowledge of the subject. Even more surprising, this was true of some who write columns and editorials on the subject of money and economics in order to inform (or mis-inform) their readers about preferred priorities in public policy. This chapter will attempt to expose readers to at least a rudimentary knowledge of what money is, and where it comes from. It is time that we removed the veil separating us from the financial holy of holies and see what the high priests of monetary orthodoxy do back there.

What is money? It is a good question for which there is no easy answer! It has meant different things to different people in different cultures in different times. Its importance was recognized in the Bible which refers to money more than seventy times. In those days money usually meant copper, silver or gold coins. An exception, and one of the earliest recorded examples of a breakdown in the monetary system, occurred during the seven-year famine recorded in Genesis. As Pharaoh's administrator, Joseph had accumulated all the money in both Egypt and Canaan in exchange for grain. But the people were still hungry so they came to Joseph and said, "Give us bread, for why should we die in your presence? For the money has failed." Joseph agreed to give them bread in exchange for livestock which became a substitute for money – an early example of mobile, liquid capital.[1]

A good example of necessity being the mother of invention.

A dual system of metallic coins and barter acted as the principal financial instruments worldwide for centuries. The first deviation from this appears to have occurred in China where they invented fei-ch'ien (flying money) which they used in a way similar to our bank drafts to send money from one place to another during the T'ang dynasty (A.D. 618-907). Later, when iron coins were the main currency in Szechuan province, the heavy weight led people to deposit them in some proto-banks and use the receipts for financial transactions. Many historians believe that the use of these receipts as a money substitute was the origin of paper money.[2]

For the next two centuries, through changing empires and dynasties, metal money coexisted with paper which had not yet become a national currency. In 1161, a new kind of money, the hui-tzu, or "check medium" was issued. It was tightly tied to reserves of copper coins so the exchange rate was kept constant for more than 20 years and it became a truly national currency around the end of the twelfth century. Then, in a situation that has been repeated innumerable times since, the government began an inflationary policy of printing money to finance two wars. The inflation starting in the second half of the twelfth century has been recorded as the first nationwide inflation of paper money in world history.[3]

THE GOLDSMITHS' SCAM

Although European banking can be traced back to Roman times my launching point is the introduction of paper money to England which appears to have begun with the London goldsmiths in the latter half of the 17th century. The next two pages from another document illustrates the profound transition in the financial system.[4,5]

THE KING HAD CONFISCATED THE GOLD AND SILVER THAT THE RICH PEOPLE HAD DEPOSITED IN THE TOWER OF LONDON, WITH NO COMPENSATION. SO THESE WEALTHY PEOPLE LOOKED AROUND FOR A SAFER PLACE TO KEEP THEIR GOLD AND SILVER...

...AND SETTLED ON THE GOLDSMITHS, WHO ALREADY HAD FIREPROOF STRONG BOXES FOR THEIR OWN VALUABLES.

THE GOLDSMITHS GAVE THEM RECEIPTS FOR THEIR DEPOSITS AND 5% INTEREST ON THE UNDERSTANDING THAT THEY COULD LEND THE MONEY OUT TO THEIR FRIENDS AT HIGHER INTEREST. THIS WAS FAIR ENOUGH, AND CONVENIENT, TOO.

INSTEAD OF GETTING THE GOLD OUT OF THE VAULT TO PAY THEIR BILLS, PEOPLE USED THE RECEIPTS FROM THE GOLDSMITHS. THE PROBLEM CAME LATER WHEN THE GOLDSMITHS FIGURED OUT THAT THEY COULD MAKE MORE LOANS THAN THEY HAD GOLD IN THEIR VAULTS. ONLY A FEW PEOPLE REDEEMED THEIR RECEIPTS FOR GOLD AT ANY ONE TIME. IF THEY HAD ALL TRIED AT ONCE THEY WOULD HAVE BEEN OUT OF LUCK BECAUSE THERE WASN'T ENOUGH GOLD TO BACK ALL THE CERTIFICATES.

IT WAS PROBABLY ILLEGAL, BUT THE GOVERNMENT BECAME AN ACCOMPLICE AND LEGALIZED THE SCAM WHEN IT CHARTERED THE BANK OF ENGLAND IN 1694.

KING WILLIAM'S WAR, 1688-1697, HAD BEEN EXTREMELY COSTLY. HE WAS SHORT OF CASH BECAUSE MOST OF HIS GOLD HAD GONE TO THE CONTINENT TO PAY FOR ARMS. SOMEONE HAD THE IDEA OF FORMING A BANK. RICH PEOPLE INVESTED £1,200,000 IN GOLD AND LENT IT TO THE GOVERNMENT AT 8%, A GOOD DEAL FOR THE BANK'S SHAREHOLDERS. TO SHOW ITS GRATITUDE, THE GOVERNMENT ALLOWED THE BANK TO PRINT 1,200,000 IN BANKNOTES TO LEND TO ITS FRIENDS.

SO THE BANK WAS ALLOWED TO LEND THE SAME MONEY TWICE. THAT WAS ONLY THE BEGINNING. OVER THE YEARS THE DEAL HAS BECOME MUCH SWEETER FOR THE BANKS.

The authority granted to the Bank of England to print bank notes, and lend them into circulation, was the beginning of what became known as the fractional reserve system. That is the practice of lending "money" that doesn't really exist. It was to become the most profitable scam in the history of humankind. It was also the quick-sand on which the Bank of England was founded in 1694.

THE BANK OF ENGLAND'S SCAM

The Bank of England had been conceived as a solution to a dilemma.King William's War, 1688-1697, had been extremely costly and this resulted in much of England's gold and silver going to the continent in payment of debt. As a result the money supply was sorely depleted and something had to be done to keep the wheels of commerce turning.

At the time the Bank was chartered, the scheme involved an initial subscription by its shareholders of £1,200,000 in gold and silver which would be lent to the government at 8 percent. That seems fair enough, although the interest rate was more than ample for a government-guaranteed investment. It was only the beginning, however, because in addition to a £4,000 management fee, the Bank of England was granted an advantage only available to banks and bankers. It was granted authority to issue "banknotes" in an amount equal to its capital and lend the notes into circulation. This was not the first case of paper money issued by private banks in the modern era, but it was the first of great and lasting significance in the English-speaking world.[6]

> Wow, it looks like a good deal for the shareholders.

> That is the story of banking.

It was the same system developed by the goldsmiths. By lending the same money twice the Bank could double the interest received on its capital. Nice work if you can get it, and you can get it with a bank charter. It was not too surprising, then, that discussions of this advantage encouraged some members of parliament to become shareholders in the Bank. Money lenders learned early, and have never forgotten, that it pays to have friends in parliament.[7]

"By the year 1725 all the basic essentials of the modern financial mechanism were in being." In England,[8] the Bank had increased its capital, its loans to the government, its issues of banknotes, and its "fractional reserves" for redeeming banknotes on demand, that is, the amount of gold the bank kept as a reserve, this being a small fraction of its outstanding banknotes. Most of the start-up problems of the bank had been disposed of and its status as a going concern firmly established. The Bank of England's unique charter gave it a virtual monopoly on banking in London.

This was not the case in other areas. By 1750 there were 12 banks outside London, and this number increased to 150 by 1776, and 721 by 1810.[9] These were called "country banks" and often they kept their reserves in banknotes of the Bank of England, rather than in gold or silver coins or ingots. As late as 1826 it was possible for Lord Liverpool to say that the law permitted any shopkeeper, however limited his means, to establish a bank ... and issue banknotes purporting to be payable on demand in Bank of England notes that were, in turn, payable by the bank in specie on demand.[10] This was a classic example of paper money backed by other paper money – in essence phony money guaranteed by phony money

This is getting more interesting all the time.

I agree, it is a fascinating story.

Meanwhile on the other side of the Atlantic Ocean both French and English colonies encountered money supply problems, and had to innovate as best possible. The French government neglected to meet the monetary needs of New France, as part of Canada was then known, and it was impossible to balance the budget with its heavy naval and military expenditures. Inflation began in 1685 when Intendant de Meulles, in great need of funds, cut playing-cards in four and signed them to serve as cash, and this card money increased in volume.[11]

GOVERNMENT-CREATED MONEY

The English colonial settlers faced comparable problems. Few were independently wealthy and the colonies suffered a chronic and often acute shortage of gold and silver coins. To make matters worse, Britain routinely banned the export of silver and gold to the colonies because it was desperately required as a base for the expansion of the money supply in the mother country. Deprived of support from "mother" England, necessity became the mother of invention.[12]

There is no doubt that the 13 colonies were the Western pioneers in the creation of "funny money," the label many skeptics and cynics apply to government-created money. Why they consider it any funnier than the phony money banks create I will never understand. Perhaps they just suffer from a peculiar sense of humor.

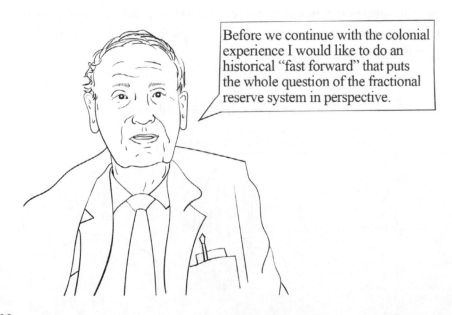

Before we continue with the colonial experience I would like to do an historical "fast forward" that puts the whole question of the fractional reserve system in perspective.

A CASE OF GLOBAL GRAND LARCENY

If banks have one thing in common it is their insatiable greed. It wasn't too long after the Bank of England was established that it became dissatisfied with a ratio of two to one, that is to lend the same money to two different borrowers, and collect interest from each. It began to lobby for an increase to three. This was the start of a campaign that continued for about three centuries.

In the early years of the 20th century, federally chartered U.S. banks had to have a gold reserve of 25 percent. That allowed them to lend the same money four times. In Canada, when I was young, banks were required to have cash reserves of 8% against deposits. That allowed Canadian banks to lend the same money 12 ½ times.

In 1991 the Canadian government of the day allowed the banks to sweet-talk it out of having any cash reserves at all. This incredible move flowed from the adoption of monetarism, the brainchild of Milton Friedman and the 2nd Chicago school of economics which espoused deregulation of the banking industry. Its implementation over three or four years cost Canadian taxpayers billions of dollars a year in lost seigniorage – the profit from printing cash money – and resulted in a multibillion dollar annual bonanza for the banks.

This policy which is now universal practice in many countries is beyond belief. The Bank for International Settlements rules allow banks a ratio of 20 to 1, compared to the 2 to 1 when the Bank of England was chartered. That means that a bank with a capital of $10 million can make loans of $200 million. At 5% those loans would earn $10 million in interest every year! That is an amount equal to its capital. Of course they have some expenses, but they are minimal, and returns of that magnitude are grand larceny!

It has resulted in a distribution in income that is beyond comprehension. A 2016 Oxfam report said that in 2010 the 88 richest people in the world owned the same wealth as the poorest 50 percent. The number of families dropped to 80 in 2014 before falling again in 2015.

"The report shows that the 62 richest people are as wealthy as half of the world's population."[13] It called for urgent action to deal with a trend showing that one percent of the people own more wealth than the other 99 percent combined. The purpose of this book is to persuade the 99% to demand a revolutionary change in the system!!!

"CHANGE THE SYSTEM NOW, OR THE PLANET WILL BURN."[14]

Twelve Shillings.

To counterfeit is *Death.*

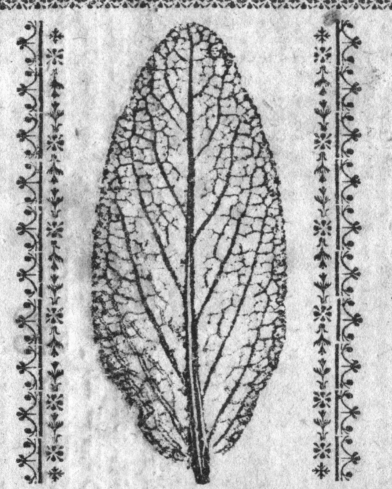

Burlington in New-Jersey,
Printed by I. Collins, 1776.

CHAPTER TWO

ENGLISH COLONISTS WERE MONETARY PIONEERS

"Everything's got a moral if you can only find it."
— Lewis Carroll

The English colonial settlers faced comparable problems. Few were independently wealthy and the colonies suffered a chronic and often acute shortage of gold and silver coins. To make matters worse, Britain routinely banned the export of silver and gold to the colonies because it was desperately required as a base for the expansion of the money supply in the mother country. Deprived of support from "mother" England, necessity became the mother of invention.[1]

In 1690, four years before the Bank of England was chartered, the Massachusetts Bay Colony issued its first colonial notes. This, according to one of my American friends, was a consequence of their part in King William's war. Soldiers had been dispatched to invade Canada on the promise that the French had lots of silver. But Quebec did not fall and the Yanks went back to Boston sore, mean, and unpaid. Something had to be done, so the Massachusetts Bay Note, redeemable in gold "sometime" was born. "This was, if not the very first, one of the first cases of government-created paper money of the modern age."[2]

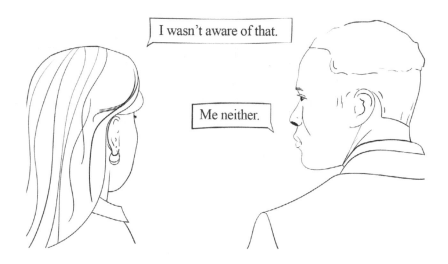

Early in the 18th century, in May 1723, Pennsylvania loaned into circulation, with real estate as security, notes to the amount of £15,000; and another £30,000 were issued in December. It was enacted that, "counterfeiters were to be punished by having both their ears cut off," being whipped on the 'bare back with thirty lashes well laid on,' and fined or sold into servitude."[3] While the punishment for counterfeiters seems somewhat extreme by 21st century standards, the issue of notes accomplished its purpose and sparked a revival of the colony's economy. Ship-building prospered and both exports and imports increased markedly.[4]

The experiment was so successful that the number of notes in circulation was increased from £15,000 in early 1723, to £81,500 in 1754 – a growth rate during the thirty-one years of a moderate 5.6 percent. Even Adam Smith, who was not a fan of government-created money, admitted that Pennsylvania's paper currency "is said never to have sunk below the value of the gold and silver which was current in the colony before the first issue of paper money."[5]

As I mentioned at the outset, the Chinese had used paper money centuries earlier, but for our part of the world, as Curtis P. Nettles points out: "Paper currency issued under government auspices originated in the thirteen colonies; and during the 18th century they were the laboratories in which many currency experiments were performed."[6] There were no banks at that time in any of the 13 colonies so all the paper money was created under the authority of the colonial legislatures. In all there were about 250 separate issues of colonial notes between 1690 and 1775 and the system worked just fine when they avoided over or under issue. It also had distinct advantages over bank or coin money. The legislature could spend, lend or transfer the money into circulation, while banks could only lend (or spend their interest earnings back into circulation) and the coin money was always leaving the colonies to pay for imports.

Historians usually play down the role of money creation as a causal factor in bringing about the War for Independence. On the other hand, "[Benjamin] Franklin cited restrictions upon paper money as one of the main reasons for the alienation of the American provinces from the mother country."[7] "To a significant extent, the war was fought over the right of the Colonists to create their own money supply. When the Continental Congress and the states brought forth large issues of their own legal-tender money in 1775, they committed acts so contrary to British laws governing the colonies and so contemptuous and insulting to British sovereignty as to make war inevitable."[8]

When the war began the United Colonies, or the United States, as they came to be called, were really strapped for gold and silver. Their difficulty was compounded by the blockade imposed by the British Navy. At the same time the war had to be financed by one means or another so the separate states, and the United States, acting through the Continental Congress in an act of defiance against King and Parliament, continued the policy that they had previously followed when gold was in short supply – they issued paper money. But now there was a difference. Instead of just printing enough to meet the needs of moderate growth in trade they had to print an amount which, when added to foreign borrowing and the receipts from taxation, was sufficient to finance the war. Inevitably that amount ceased to have any relation to the increase in output of goods and services and the paper began to lose its value. In 1784 Benjamin Franklin, after defending the necessity of what was done, went on to explain the consequences of excess. "It has been long and often observed, that when the current money of a country is augmented beyond the occasions for money as a medium of commerce, its value as money diminishes..."[9]

A classic case of printing too much money and creating inflation.

It is a truism to which one can say Amen! The amount of money created, was so great that its worthlessness, was inevitable.

It is noteworthy, however, that much of the hyperinflation of the later years of the Revolution was caused by British counterfeiting in a deliberate attempt to discredit the Continental currency. If that was their aim they succeeded brilliantly but in this particular round of the war over money it was the colonies that had the last laugh. They paid for much of their war effort by issuing "funny" money and the total cost, including interest, until the debt was liquidated, has been estimated as about $250 million. Britain, on the other hand, relied almost entirely on "phony" bank-created borrowed money. "By 1783, the British national debt was roughly $500 million greater than in 1774. But here is the really interesting fact: Britain's national debt has never since 1783 been less than it was at the end of that year."[10] The conclusion that William Hixson draws in his excellent book the Triumph of the Bankers (which should be required reading for every student of monetary policy) is that "Britain has not even yet finished paying for the war it lost attempting to suppress the emerging United States."[11] Hixson goes on to say that in the intervening 200 years British taxpayers have paid over $4 billion in interest to their moneylending class of 1783 and its heirs. To add injury to insult, the original $500 million is still outstanding.[12]

While Americans won that round, future historians may speculate about who "lost" the next one. As a result of the hyperinflation, and the discredited "Continental", Alexander Hamilton, who seemed determined to model the United States monetary and banking system on that of England, was able to get a federal charter for the first Bank of the United States (BUS) and several state banks were chartered. This took place despite the strongly expressed views of Benjamin Franklin, John Adams, and Thomas Jefferson. The Jeffersonians hated the BUS and had it killed after 20 years. Meanwhile the United States didn't create any legal tender paper money from the Revolution until Lincoln's Greenbacks, but this over-reaction exacted a heavy price.

The years immediately following the War for Independence were not happy ones for the people of the United States. The collapse of the monetary system, and the absence of sufficient gold and silver to facilitate trade, caused the country to experience its first great depression. Debtors, who had been able to pay creditors with cheap money during the inflationary period, now had to pay with money that was scarce and therefore dear. Thus, as Richard B. Morris explains, "each one of the thirteen states found creditors arrayed against debtors."[13] The depression constituted the second half of the lesson in monetary theory. Whereas too much money leads to inflation, too little leads to economic paralysis. Unfortunately these inalienable truths proved to be an insufficient guide for future policy makers.

For almost a hundred years following the War for Independence arguments about "money questions" and the role of banks raged on. Myriad new state banks appeared but when the United States declared war on Britain on June 18, 1812, the task of financing the conflict was considerably more difficult due to the absence of any sort of "central bank". Gold had to be exported to pay for armaments and hoarding was rampant; so except for a few banks in New England most were forced to suspend redemption of their notes on demand, and convertibility was not re-instated until February 1817.[14]

Meanwhile the banking industry was not unaware of the opportunity this presented on the financial side of the economy. The number of banks in the U.S. increased from 30, in 1800, to 713 by 1836. By then they had created $306 million in banknotes, plus deposits, but had only about $40 million in gold in their vaults. The ratio for the banks total liabilities – bank notes plus deposits – to metallic reserves was just about seven and a half to one.[15]

Although regulation of the banks was inadequate or non-existent some banks followed very conservative reserve policies. Others, however, did not! An extreme example is provided by the Farmers' Exchange Bank of Gloucester (Rhode Island), founded in 1804. An investigating committee of the state legislature found that on the basis of only $3 million capital stock in gold, by 1809 the bank had loaned into circulation banknotes it had itself created to the total amount of $580 million. In other words it had only sufficient reserves to liquidate about half a cent for every dollar of its obligations.[16]

I have never heard of a scam like that.

Well, you have now.

It was the Civil War, however, which had the biggest impact on the system. Once again gold was in short supply so the banks suspended payment making the issue of United States Notes [greenbacks] unavoidable. Although the need was to meet the exigencies of war there had long been a need for a "universal," or national currency to replace the hodgepodge existing at the time. One historian estimated that in 1860 there were "7,000 kinds of paper notes in circulation, not to mention 5,000 counterfeit issues."[17]

VICTORY OF THE BANKERS

From the time greenbacks first came into circulation in 1862 they carried the words: "The United States of America will pay to the bearer five dollars … payable at the United States Treasury." In fact, however, they were government-created inconvertible money until 1879 when they first became convertible into gold at face value. Convertibility was introduced by Hugh McCulloch, a former banker and gold monometallist who became secretary of the treasury in 1865. He agreed with his old buddies in the banking fraternity that steps should be taken to make greenbacks convertible into gold as soon as possible. Since there were hundreds of millions of dollars in paper outstanding at the time, and little gold in the treasury with which to redeem it, McCulloch concluded that it would be easier to reduce the number of greenbacks than to increase the gold in the treasury. So he sold bonds in exchange for greenbacks and then destroyed the greenbacks. In other words he exchanged interest-bearing debt for non-interest bearing debt.[18] It is interesting to speculate what might have happened had McCulloch been a farmer or businessman. In any event, he decided to emulate mother England by putting the country in debt. There is little doubt that it was the bankers and moneylenders who won that round.

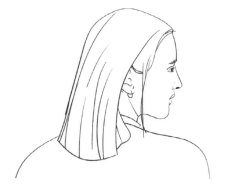

THE GOLD STANDARD – ANOTHER WRONG TURN

O f the three categories of monetary enthusiasts, those who preferred gold-backed currency, those who were quite willing to settle for silver-backed, and those who preferred no metal backing at all, it was ultimately the monometallists or gold standard supporters who carried the day. The gold standard was a commitment by participating countries to fix the prices of their domestic currencies in terms of a specific amount of gold – a practice followed in various European countries from time to time. "England adopted a de facto gold standard in 1717 ... and formally adopted the gold standard in 1819."[19] Convertibility was suspended during the Napoleonic War and re-instated in 1821, at the urging of economist David Ricardo, and others, at the pre-war rate of exchange.

"The United States, though formally on a bimetallic (gold and silver) standard switched to gold *de facto* in 1834 and *de jure* in 1900. Other major countries joined the gold standard in the 1870's. The period from 1880 to 1914 is known as the classical gold standard.[20] Eventually it became an international standard. It had to be abandoned during wartime as a matter of expediency. Later, when economic activity returned to normal, there was always pressure for its re-instatement.

The classical attachment to the gold standard was so strong that even the redoubtable Winston Churchill was captive of its orthodoxy. As Chancellor of the Exchequer, he was largely responsible for England's return to the gold standard at the old parity after World War I. In his Budget speech of April 28, 1925, he declared: "A return to the gold standard has long been a settled and declared policy of this country. Every Expert Conference since the war ... has urged in principle the return to the gold standard. No responsible authority has advocated any other policy."[21]

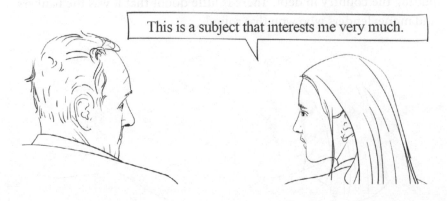

This is a subject that interests me very much.

Churchill stressed that in addition to those countries that had already returned to the gold standard there should be simultaneous action by Holland, the Dutch East Indies, Australia and New Zealand. Some other countries used U.S. dollars or British pounds as reserves on the basis that those currencies were convertible into gold and consequently they could be considered an acceptable substitute for gold. Churchill described the advantage of this common international action in the following metaphor: "That standard [the gold standard] may of course vary in itself from time to time, but the position of all countries related to it will vary together like ships in a harbour whose gangways are joined and who rise and fall together with the tide."[22]

Churchill based his case primarily on the Report of the Committee on the Currency and the Bank of England Note Issues. The arguments of the Committee were brief and clear as far as they went, although they were described as jejune (devoid of substance) by J.M. Keynes. They never explored the general desirability of a gold standard from the point of view of the interests of the different social classes affected by its operation. The general advantages of a gold standard were not stated by the report, but were taken for granted as self-evident. So much for the opinions of "experts."

In retrospect one wonders why support of the gold standard was so deeply entrenched. It was obvious that every time gold went out of the country to pay for imports, the money supply contracted and this had a negative effect on the domestic economy. On the other hand when gold was received in payment for exports the money supply increased rapidly and inflation took hold. This uncritical attachment to the gold standard must have had something to do with mysticism or its long romantic history as a prize worthy of kings and buccaneers. As an economic regulator, however, it was an abomination.

39

It is difficult for me to credit that such an absurd system would last until August 15, 1971, when President Richard Nixon announced that the United States would no longer redeem currency held by foreign central banks for gold. This action was the last gasp of the gold standard. It is even more difficult to believe, as Michael D. Bordo says in his essay on the Gold Standard in the *Encyclopaedia of Economics*: "Widespread dissatisfaction with high inflation in the late seventies and early eighties brought renewed interest in the gold standard."[23] If true, and I am cynical enough to accept that it is, it only proves that some economists are incapable of learning.

It makes little difference to most of us how much gold our income will buy. What concerns us is the kind of "basket" of goods and services that Irving Fisher wrote about and which is now the basis for a consumer price index. How much food, clothing, and shelter will our paycheck buy and will there be anything left over for dinner out and family vacations? Also a few years from now, after we retire? These are the variables that we hope will be constant, on average, not how many gold or silver wafers we can buy with our dollars, pounds or euros. It is the package of goods and services that these currencies can be exchanged for which determines their value.

CHAPTER THREE

THE BUBBLE ECONOMY

"The definition of insanity is doing the same thing over and over again and expecting different results."
– Albert Einstein

I had intended to have this chapter later in the book but the totally grotesque and unprecedented events of the last few days have propelled it to center stage. The Coronavirus disease also known as COVID-19 has unraveled our globalized economy and left it in a shambles that portends yet another world-wide recession.

The depth and magnitude of the crisis was underlined for me when I opened my front door to pick up our newspaper on Friday March 20, the first full day of Spring 2020. Our neighbor's door is only about four feet from ours and they subscribe to a different paper, The *National Post*. I couldn't help but see its more dramatic headline in large bold letters: ECHOES OF THE THIRTIES.

That did it. That's where I came in. I was born in the twenties and grew up in the dirty thirties when I had seen poverty in its rawest form. Our farm home was close to the Cockshutt Road running from Brantford, Ontario, Canada, south to Lake Erie, one of the Great Lakes. Regularly, poor men who would be walking down the road, would knock at our door and ask for food. My saintly mother would invariably give them a good hot meal before they went on their way.

It was a time when unemployed men would attempt to hitch a ride in an empty railway boxcar until they were intercepted by the police whose orders from the government did not mention the word compassion. The depth of the poverty was so great that my cousin John Bertran, an insurance salesman who later became the "best man" at my wedding, wore out the soles of his shoes and he couldn't afford to have them half-soled; but, instead, he used cardboard to protect his feet from the elements.

These images had a profound impact on my psyche; so much so that after I was discharged from military service in 1946, I took advantage of veteran benefits and enrolled in the University of Toronto where economics was my subject of greatest interest. When I asked my professors if recessions and depressions were necessary, I found their answers very unsatisfactory. In effect they assured me that business cycles occurred periodically and were endemic to our economic system. Regrettably professors of Economics are still saying the same thing having learned it by rote.

I was not amused! It was like saying that a beautiful car that could cruise along the highway at sixty miles an hour, but would occasionally slowed to forty, was designed that way. If true, it is a faulty design and should be fixed! Centuries ago, the monarchs created all of the money and it was put into circulation debt free. After a long battle that right was transferred to the people as represented by their governments. A small group of cunning and sometimes ruthless individuals persuaded governments to delegate the creation of money to them.

But, there was a catch. Instead of creating our money free of debt as the monarchs had, they would create it as debt. They would give us "money," but we had to agree to pay it back with interest. But with no one creating any money with which to repay either principal or interest, our only recourse was to keep on borrowing and going deeper and deeper into debt to people who have been able to amass fortunes so large they are beyond comprehension.

Before I continue it is necessary to say that the people working in the banking industry are ordinary, decent people who treat us well and provide us with essential services. So in most cases they are blameless and many are to be praised. I know from speaking to many of them that they don't have a clue about the larger picture.

ONE GIANT PONZI SCHEME

The world financial system is a total fraud. It is one gargantuan Ponzi scheme, no better than the one Bernie Madoff used to swindle his friends and neighbors, and thousands of times worse if you add up the total number of victims it has ripped off over countless generations.

The principal difference between the two schemes is that Madoff was acting outside the law while the international banking cartel has persuaded generation after generation of monarchs, presidents and prime ministers to provide legislative protection for their larceny.

The banks' Ponzi scheme is alarmingly simple. They lend the same money to several people or institutions at the same time and collect interest on it from each. What the banks really lend, however, is their credit, and what they take back in compensation for that privilege is a debt that must be repaid with interest.[1]

A BONANZA FOR THE BANKERS, BUT A DEAD END FOR THE WORLD ECONOMY. MORE THAN THREE HUNDRED YEARS OF LEGAL ROBBERY MUST END NOW!

THE BUBBLE / BALLOON ECONOMY

Our incredibly disastrous banking and financial system can be likened to a balloon. When there is a demand for "money" to implement a new invention like railways, commercial airplanes, defense expenditures, a housing backlog or just a stream of financial optimism, the banks will create large amounts of credit and the economy grows like a balloon being pumped full of air. Then if for any one of many reasons including a Coronavirus lockdown, or an oil price slugging match between two stubborn regimes, the economy will begin to collapse.

Credit for marginal or outdated industries will begin to dry up. People laid off from their jobs will become credit risks. Inevitably the credit balloon will begin to shrink like a balloon with a pin stuck in it. In effect the money (virtual) supply will shrink because it is just like filling wheelbarrows with money and shoveling it into a fiery furnace. Austerity will reign as budgets are shrunk to match the new reduced money supply.

If the unprecedented events of 2020 result in a recession, and austerity economics, it won't be the first time. There were fourteen recessions and depressions in the U.S. between the Great Depression of 1929-1939 and the Great Recession of 2008 to 2018. None of them was necessary! Every one was due to our stubborn adherence to a banking system based almost exclusively on hot air (credit) rather than legal tender. The result has been human distress and hardship that is incalculable. The loss in output due to so many periods of operating the world economy below its physical capacity has also been incalculable. Many, many trillions of value lost forever.

A FEW OF THE BURSTING BUBBLES
The Great Depression 1929-1939

Although I was a child of the Depression, and saw human suffering on a scale that I hoped never to see again, I was too young to be aware that it was the New York banks that were the villains responsible. Their moral depravity, in tandem with political naivety, were responsible for the tragedy.

In the 1920s the New York banks had abandoned the rules that had applied to legitimate banks and became scam artists and stock market manipulators. They encouraged individuals and corporations to buy stocks on margin, i.e. with just a small down payment, and established the kind of investment fever that led inevitably to the crash of 1929. All of the big banks were players in this tragic opera with J. P. Morgan and Co. playing a key role.

If you want to read the whole script, I would recommend getting a copy of *The Trouble with Billionaires* by Linda McQuaig & Neil Brooks. "By 1933, there were thirteen million unemployed (about 25% of the labor force), with thousands of homeless men riding the rails searching for work. The enraged American public was not only hungry for food, but also hungry for answers about what had gone so terribly wrong".[2]

Soon after Franklin Roosevelt became president, the U.S. Senate Banking and Currency Committee set up a commission to investigate the banks' role in the worst crash in which the banks had been involved. They hired a former New York assistant attorney general, Ferdinand Pecora, to lead the charge. Pecora was relentless and uncompromising. The kind of investigator who leaves no stone unturned. His damning report showing that the big New York banks had been rotten to the core, became known as the Pecora Report.

In June 1933 President Roosevelt signed an historic bill sponsored by Senator Carter Glass and Representative Henry Steagall. What became known as the Glass-Steagall Act restored the division between banks that take deposits from the public and those that are allowed to trade in the stock market with its well-known volatility. As you might guess it was only a matter of time before the banks began to lobby the president and the Congress to remove the restrictions that had protected depositors for decades and let them back into the financial casinos. Pity!

The Recession of 1981-82

If the first quarter century after World War II moved along smoothly the same cannot be said for the second quarter century. A dramatic change occurred which was not sustainable in the long run. Prices of goods and services began to creep up and this inflationary trend became a matter of increasing concerns in official circles.

We were told that beginning sometime during the 1970s "Central Bankers in leading countries, including the United States, no longer offered a laundry list of important objectives. They began to describe their principal task as the maintenance of price stability."[3] That is interesting information! Who made the decision? Congress? Parliament? I knew dozens of politicians in several countries and I cannot recall a single conversation in which one of them said: "Guess what? We have decided to concentrate on inflation and forget about unemployment." Perhaps I wasn't listening, but as one familiar with how the system works I would guess that this decision was taken by bureaucrats and bankers, people who normally can survive a recession without losing their jobs. They would then "advise" governments overly dependent on their advice.

In any event, that's how the cookie crumbled. At the outset of the '80s Fed Chairman Paul Volcker in the U.S., and his equivalents in several other countries, decided to give their economies a good thrashing. Apparently Volcker and the other central bankers had not learned from the 1970 and 1975 recessions that monetarily-induced reductions in inflation rates were only temporary. Instead they must have concluded that the failure of those earlier tests could be attributed to a lack of will. The contractions hadn't been sufficiently long or sufficiently severe. So, steeped in the monetarist theology, they decided to carry the 1981-82 experiment to its logical conclusion – presumably zero inflation. Before reaching that target, however, it became obvious that they might succeed in collapsing the whole Western monetary system. Either prudence or fright caused them to turn off their death machines just in time to prevent a catastrophe worldwide.

It was too late, however, to prevent both financial and social disaster. Paul Volcker in the U.S., and Bank of Canada Governor Gerald Bouey in Canada were heroes with the business and financial tycoons. In the real world, however, as they pushed interest rates to a high of 18 percent in the U.S., and a sky-high 22 percent in Canada, the action they took was comparable to using a bulldozer to weed a vegetable garden. The result was a combined financial and social disaster.

As unemployment increased, and individuals paid less in taxes, governments had to borrow to make up the deficit and pay ridiculously high interest rates on the money they borrowed. On the social side millions of people lost their jobs, their homes, their farms and their businesses as their dreams of the good life were snuffed out by a few people whose names they barely knew.

Just as most people are not really aware of how banks create money, by creating deposits, they are equally unfamiliar with the opposite action. Banks destroy money (credit) when they call loans. The Fed decides to sell a bond for cash or its equivalent. The amount of high-powered money, as it was known at that time, was reduced by the amount of the transaction. This required the banks to reduce their loans outstanding by an equivalent amount multiplied by their leverage. It was a chain reaction. When the system is expanding, it is like a balloon. When it is contracting the system acts like a balloon with a pin stuck in it, i.e. a recession or depression.

I know that someone will argue, as the President's Council of Economic Advisers did in February 1983, that the very sharp decline in 1982 did not reflect a decrease in the growth of the monetary aggregates. "Rather an exceptional severity of the slowdown in nominal GNP growth can be traced to a combination of factors that led to an unusually sharp decline in the velocity of money, that is, in the ratio of GNP to the money stock."[4]

What did they expect? Faced with staggering unemployment people with jobs decided it was prudent to hang on to their money in case their pink slip was next. So for a number of reasons, including fear and uncertainty of the future, the velocity of money declined and the U.S. sank into the deepest recession in fifty years. As always, it was the poor who suffered most. As Isabel V. Sawhill wrote in her essay on "Poverty in the United States" for the *Encyclopedia of Economics*: "Researchers have found that recessions have a disproportionate impact on the poor because they cause rising unemployment, a reduction in work hours, and the stagnation of family incomes. The link between macroeconomic conditions and the incidence of poverty was clearly visible during the 1982 recession, when the poverty rate rose to 15.2 percent, up from 13.0 percent in 1980."[5]

The callous attitude of the Fed and other central banks was, in a sense, legitimized by the notion of a natural rate of unemployment defined as the lowest rate of unemployment tolerable without pushing up inflation. This idea, advanced by Milton Friedman and Edmund Phelps, has been a great disservice to both economic theory and performance. Specifically, it has directed attention away from an attempt to find the reasons for the increased inflation that began in the mid-'60s by making an unnatural situation sound normal instead of abnormal.

I recall addressing a class of university students some years ago on the subject of contemporary inflation and telling them how a common sense incomes policy would wrestle it to the ground. In the question period that followed a young man rose, and with that combination of brashness, irreverence and sarcasm of which I might have been guilty at the same age, asked if I had not heard of the "natural rate of unemployment?" I was not sure that I had because it was just a new invention – an excuse to cover the economists' lack of understanding of the origin of stagflation.

In an interview with Nobel laureate Gunnar Myrdal, who claimed credit for coining the word stagflation, he admitted that he didn't understand what caused it. My thesis, which will be elaborated in a later chapter, is that stagflation resulted from the irresponsible use of monopoly power on the part of big labor and big business. Wage settlements were negotiated that were well in excess of productivity increases. Labor unit costs rose, followed by prices. Central banks were put in the invidious position of having to print enough money to clear the market at the new higher price levels, which would bring roaring inflation, or of refusing to finance the process which would produce massive unemployment at the same time – hence "stagflation".

Inventing a "natural rate" of unemployment, about which there is nothing natural at all, was an attempt to rationalize the phenomenon. In the process it became a license for central banks to pursue inhumane and irrational policies.

Just step back a pace or two and take a clear look at what they did. In 1981-82 the Fed in the U.S., and central banks in other countries, deliberately put millions of people out of work. The ranks of the unemployed swelled to 30 million in the Western world. Then governments everywhere began to scramble around and introduce new programs of every type and description to try to re-employ a few of them. Can you imagine anything more brilliantly insane than one arm of government extinguishing millions of jobs while other arms, at considerable cost to taxpayers, try to create a few thousands to fill the void? It is comparable to deliberately torpedoing a ship load of passengers and then sending a few lifeboats to rescue a minority of the stragglers.

A SECOND STUPID RECESSION

We hadn't fully recovered from the effects of the 1981-82 recession when the spin doctors who control our destiny decided to give us another massive injection of their pain producer. We were told, of course, that it would just be short-term pain necessary to restore the economy to full health – to " re-establish the fundamentals", as they call it.

Why, when they have used the same medicine at least half a dozen times in the course of the last forty years and the fundamentals aren't right yet, would anyone believe them? When a Liberal government allowed the Bank of Canada to sabotage the Canadian economy in 1981-82 the Progressive Conservative opposition finance critic, Mike Wilson, is alleged to have said: "This is insane." A decade later, as Minister of Finance, the same Wilson defended the Bank's repeat performance - even more ruinous than the one he had labeled as "insane".

In reality, politicians have become little more than talking heads. In opposition they criticize, often with much justice, the financial policies of the government. Then the sides change and the roles reverse. It is a phenomenon I understand only too well from personal experience. The so-called "expert" advisers get politicians in closed rooms and brief them fervently. They call the meetings "information briefings" but often the real object of the exercise is intimidation. Their purpose is to persuade the politicians that their natural instincts are wrong and that the experts are right and that non-compliance could lead to some financial disaster for which "you, Mr. Secretary" or "you, Minister" would be held responsible. It is difficult, bordering on impossible, to stand up to that kind of pressure. Instead, most politicians get stuck with accepting the consequences of taking advice from experts who, all too often, are the kind of experts who have all the answers without necessarily being familiar with the problems. The tragedy of the last few decades is that the consequences of official advice have rendered politicians impotent to cope with people's real problems and this has undermined confidence in the efficacy of the political system and, of course, of politicians themselves.

The fallout from what I consider bad advice has been enormous. While discussion of the disadvantages for the poor and those who lose their jobs has been widespread, less has been said about the side effects on business and government. Each recession produces a fresh wave of bankruptcies and many of the victims are innocents who would have no way of knowing that an unexpected restriction or reduction in their line of credit, at a critical juncture of their development, could turn their dreams into a nightmare of insolvency.

Even less talked about are the effects of high interest rates on those businesses that weathered the storm. Higher interest rates increased costs and cut into profits in an environment where it was difficult to raise prices enough to cover the increased tribute to the money lenders. While non-financial corporate profits before-interest-payments remained reasonably constant from 1952 to 1988, the after-interest-payment profits fell by half from about 10% of GDP to approximately 5% with the steepest decline occurring in the early 1980s when the Fed pushed interest rates through the roof.

IT WAS THE FAULT OF THE CENTRAL BANKERS

Central bankers believed that the real economy was the same one they had read about in their textbooks. Inflation was the result of too much money chasing too few goods in a market economy. Alas the market economy of the textbooks didn't exist in the real world of political economies, where many of the most important prices were set by monopolies, oligopolies and labor unions.

For more than a quarter of a century I had argued that the principal cause of contemporary inflation in Western industrialized economies was nominal wage increases being out-of-joint with productivity. Oil shocks and other price changes produce blips but the trend line is determined by the gap between nominal wages and real output.

Most economists recognize that there is a relationship between wages and prices. The President's Council of Economic Advisers was right on target in its 1981 report in stating: "... since payments to labor are estimated to account for almost two-thirds of total production costs, prices over the long term tend to move in conjunction with changes in labor unit costs."[6]

Precisely! In the longer term, prices move up at a rate that approximates the increase in wages and fringe benefits minus the increase in real output per person.

POST KOREAN WAR INFLATION: $\dot{P} = \dot{W} - \bar{\dot{Q}}$[7]

The data support the proposition as closely as anything in economics. The rate of change in the price level will approximate the difference between the average rate of change in money wages, including fringe benefits, and the average rate of change in the production of goods and services. Stating this symbolically, we have $\dot{P} = \dot{W} - \bar{\dot{Q}}$ where $\dot{P}$ is the rate of change in the price level, $\dot{W}$ is the average rate of change in money wages, and $\bar{\dot{Q}}$ is the average rate of real output of goods and services per worker in the labor force.

The assumptions include reasonable levels of employment. The definition varies from country to country, but for my purposes it is the condition that would be considered "normal" at the time. Another condition is a neutral monetary policy. This assumes that the money stock will be changed at a rate that will neither "overheat" nor "cool" the economy. The third assumption is that domestic prices are not unduly influenced by imports – that in fact import prices are rising at a rate more or less comparable to domestic prices.

Of course, $\dot{P} = \dot{W} - \bar{Q}$ is an imprecise formula – especially in the short run – because its accuracy depends on assumptions that seldom apply for extended periods. But if one looks at the data for a group of fifteen O.E.C.D. (Organization for Economic Co-operation and Development) countries shown in Table 1, the long-term result for most countries is close. The over-all average of averages is amazingly accurate – within one-quarter of one percent over a 27-year period.[8] A correlation that close is very convincing!

Table 1 [9]

Average Growth Rates of
Prices, Wages, and Productivity for 15 O.E.C.D. Countries
($\dot{W}, \bar{Q}$ calculated per Member of the Labour Force), 1964-1991

	(1) $\dot{P}$	(2) $\dot{W}$	(3) $\bar{Q}$	(4) $\dot{W}\text{-}\bar{Q}$	(5) (1)-(4)
Austria	4.3	7.7	3.0	4.7	-0.4
Belgium	5.0	7.7	2.6	5.1	-0.1
Canada	5.6	7.1	1.3	5.8	-0.2
Denmark	6.6	8.5	1.5	7.0	-0.4
France	6.3	9.2	2.5	6.7	-0.4
Germany	3.3	6.4	2.4	4.0	-0.7
Ireland	8.2	11.3	3.3	8.0	0.2
Italy	8.5	11.9	2.9	9.0	-0.5
Japan	5.2	9.5	4.4	5.1	0.1
Netherlands	4.6	6.3	1.5	4.8	-0.2
Norway	6.6	8.3	2.3	6.0	0.6
Sweden	6.9	8.9	1.7	7.2	-0.3
Switzerland	3.9	6.4	1.5	4.9	-1.0
U.K.	7.7	9.4	1.8	7.6	0.1
U.S.	5.2	6.0	0.8	5.2	0.0
Aggregate Average	5.85	8.29	2.23	6.07	-0.22

Source: Q, W – OECD National Accounts;
P=CPI in IMF Financial Statistics Yearbook
Labour Force – OECD Labour Force Statistics

It may be of interest to note that this was the fourth time that I had this table prepared for various periods beginning in 1958, and the correlation has always been of the same order of magnitude.

THE ALTERNATIVE

If the central bankers had done their homework they would have realized that the inflationary problem they had to contend with was not the one they had learned from the textbooks. It was not too much money chasing too few goods! There was no shortage of goods, store shelves were well stocked and warehouses were full. The problem was wages rising out of sync with productivity.

All they had to do was invoke a 12 to 14 month wage and price freeze applying to all goods and services, except fresh produce from the farms and the fisherman's catch from the sea where genuine markets existed. The result at the end of the period would have been zero inflation, much better than the results obtained by Paul Volcker and his cohort.

Not only that, there would not have been any massive unemployment, loss of homes, farms and businesses, and governments wouldn't have suffered serious loss of revenue that had to be made up by borrowing at exorbitant interest rates. That was a rational solution if the bankers had only taken off their academic blinders and looked for it.

AN
INQUIRY

INTO THE

NATURE AND CAUSES

OF THE

WEALTH OF NATIONS.

BY

ADAM SMITH, LL. D.

AND F. R. S. OF LONDON AND EDINBURGH:

ONE OF THE COMMISSIONERS OF HIS MAJESTY'S CUSTOMS IN
SCOTLAND;

AND FORMERLY PROFESSOR OF MORAL PHILOSOPHY
IN THE UNIVERSITY OF GLASGOW.

IN THREE VOLUMES.

VOL. I.

A NEW EDITION.

PHILADELPHIA:

PRINTED FOR THOMAS DOBSON, AT THE STONE
HOUSE, IN SECOND STREET.

MDCCLXXXIX.

CHAPTER FOUR

A PLETHORA OF IDEAS

"Economics is extremely useful as a form of employment for economists."
– J.K. Galbraith

A ny serious look at economic history has to begin with Adam Smith. He was born in Kirkcaldy, Scotland, and inherited many of the traits and attitudes sometimes attributed to the Scots. He was educated at the University of Glasgow and then Balliol College at Oxford. Following graduation he returned home to teach at the University of Glasgow where he held first the Chair of Ethics and then the Chair of Moral Philosophy in 1752.

Following a two-year stint as a tutor, he returned home to write *The Wealth of Nations*, published in 1776, the same year the American Declaration of Independence was signed. Smith's book was to become a kind of bible of economic thought.

"To Smith sympathy and self-interest were not antithetical; they were complementary. 'Man has almost constant occasion for the help of his brethren, and it is in vain for him to expect it from their benevolence only,' he explained in *The Wealth of Nations*."[1]

"Charity, while a virtuous act, could not alone provide the essentials for living. Self-interest was the mechanism that could remedy this short-coming. Said Smith. 'It is not from the benevolence of the butcher, the brewer, or the baker, that we can expect our dinner, but from their regard to their own interest.'"[2]

Smith's understanding of human nature is dead on. Entrepreneurs have been a powerful force in economics but they expect to benefit from their effort and the risk they take. But Smith realized that they can't do it all alone. Governments should provide the infrastructure and make the rules. It has to be a team effort.

While entrepreneurs and business in general are quite happy and often quite demanding that governments provide the necessary infrastructure, they are less happy and often quite violently opposed to rules that require them to produce and sell nutritious food, automobiles that are safe to drive, and buildings strong enough to remain standing even when rocked by an unexpected earthquake.

In recent years there have been increasing demands for self-regulation that have led to tragic results from inadequate standards and cutting corners on maintenance. Poor standards are justified by a school of laissez-faire counting on the "invisible hand" attributed to Adam Smith in an era that has very little resemblance to the one in which we live. The only "invisible hand" that I have seen is that of the chartered banks picking the pockets of the poor.

One rule that became obvious centuries ago was a prohibition of entrepreneurs combining to form giant firms and oligopolies capable of evading anti-trust legislation and of forming cartels that are capable of setting prices and operating by their own rules. This is the new world that we have to cope with. Some visionaries, like Dr. David Korton, saw it coming and wrote about it in his book *When Corporations Rule the World*.[3]

The giant corporations have been following practices that are hurtful to the lives and liberty of the majority, although there is beginning to be a backlash against junk food, sugar drinks and support for a continuation of the oil economy at the cost of making the planet uninhabitable. All of these are on what might be regarded as the supply side of the economy. An even more urgent problem is the distribution of the vast wealth that is being produced. Why is there inadequate money to meet the bare needs of the majority? Why is it controlled by the most powerful group on Earth? That is the subject we are exploring here.

MORE HISTORY

The roaring 20s (1920s) proved to be the catalyst that led to one of the greatest financial tragedies in history. The banks, as you might expect, were the principal actors. They tired of their legitimate functions of guarding their depositors' money, and allocating it to the needs of a rapidly expanding industrial economy. They wanted bigger returns from all manner of schemes and scams that were far more exciting.

"The nation's leading banks, liberated by President Taft from their legal responsibility to stay out of the world of gambling, had jumped in fully. Their presence only helped drive the frenzy. After all, the major Wall Street banks seemed to know what they were doing. So, for instance, the public was inclined to trust the National City Company, a securities affiliate of the powerful National City Bank, which was controlled by Rockefeller with a major share held by J.P. Morgan. At the height of the boom,

National City Company had some 1,900 salesmen out aggressively selling its financial products, including some highly risky Latin American loans that were offered to the public as largely risk-free bonds. Whereas potential investors would have likely been skeptical of bonds offered by unknown dealers from Brazil, Chile, or Peru, they put aside such fears and eagerly bought up the near-worthless bonds when they were offered by an affiliate of the prestigious National City Bank, with its top-drawer Wall Street pedigree.[4]

"The banks were only too pleased to take advantage of such trusting naïveté, selling shares in investment trusts to the investing public at greatly inflated prices. In 1927, the public bought more than $400 million worth of stock in investment trusts; in 1929, that number rose to $3 billion. The ultimate scam, launched in the final gasp of market frenzy leading up to the crash, involved a Morgan-sponsored investment trust known as Alleghany Corporation selling shares in a holding company that went on a massive binge of railroad and real-estate takeovers.[5] The company created a giant pyramid scheme in which each new purchase was used as collateral for the next."[6]

The above two paragraphs are taken from *The Trouble with Billionaires*, by Linda McQuaig and Neil Brooks, an absolutely brilliant exposé of the skullduggery practiced by the rich elite.

Eventually, as was inevitable, the bubble burst, and the whole world suffered immeasurably. By 1933, there were thirteen million unemployed in the U.S. and the contagion spread to Canada. In both countries there were countless men riding the rails looking for work and food. The outrage was universal.

When Franklin D. Roosevelt was president, he established a hearing that produced what I usually refer to as the Pecora Report. This tough, no nonsense, former New York assistant attorney general took the banks on for size and in this case, he won. The Senate Banking and Currency Committee that sponsored the investigation, retained Ferdinand Pecora to expose the depth of the skullduggery perpetrated by the most powerful men in America, and their total contempt for the interests of the small investor.

THE SEARCH FOR SOLUTIONS

Following a wound so deep, there were many men and women who dedicated their time and effort searching for a solution that would prevent a repetition of the Great Depression from ever happening again. In June 1933, President Roosevelt signed the *Glass-Steagall Act* sponsored by Senator Carter Glass and Representative Henry Steagall. This Act restored the strict wall of separation between investment banking and commercial banking in order to protect the savings and deposits of the public. A few decades later the cunning banks remembered some old tricks and persuaded a naïve Congress, unfamiliar with their own financial history, to repeal the *Glass-Steagall Act* and give the big banks back their licenses to gamble and use their money power to the disadvantage of the small players.

JOHN MAYNARD KEYNES

J.M. Keynes was an Englishman who was one of the most controversial economists of his day. Born in Cambridge, he attended King's College, Cambridge, where he earned a degree in mathematics in 1905. He obtained celebrity status when he wrote his book *The Economic Consequences of the Peace* where he objected to the punitive reparation payments imposed on Germany after World War I. The amounts demanded by the Allies were so large, he thought, that a Germany required to pay them would be perpetually poor and, consequently, politically unstable. History proved that Keynes was right.

In my opinion he erred at the 1944 Bretton Woods Conference where the International Monetary Fund was established to play a role in supporting a system of fixed exchange rates. This was a huge error in judgement by the system's promoters. The value of a nation's currency in comparison to that of any other nation is just another price that can change dramatically with changing circumstances. The attempt to maintain a parity was as futile as trying to push water uphill.

It was Keynes' reaction to the high level of unemployment between World War I and World War II that led to his greatest triumph. He introduced the notion of aggregate demand as the sum of consumption, investment and government spending. Next, he suggested that governments should undertake deficit spending to maintain full employment in times of economic turndown. He developed these themes in his seminal work, *The General Theory of Employment, Interest and Money*.

Keynes believed that once full employment was achieved the market would operate normally and all would be well. The implied assumption was that once the economy was up to speed it would be possible to not only balance budgets but to generate a surplus that could be used to repay the borrowed money that had provided the stimulus in the first place.

Alas, there was a missing link in the equation. The first part worked but there was no second part. As the labor force grows, productivity increases and wages rise. There is not enough money in circulation to clear the market so governments are faced with a choice between austerity budgets and renewed unemployment, or continued borrowing to supplement the "aggregate demand" at the expense of adding to the debt that can never be repaid.

EVEN MORE RADICAL IDEAS

Keynes' band-aid solution was much more conventional than other ideas spawned by the Great Depression. At the University of Chicago, the Economics Department produced some cutting-edge proposals. Henry Simons and Lloyd Mints questioned the whole notion behind the partial reserve system of banking. They proposed that it should be replaced with one where bank deposits were 100% backed by government-created money. Obviously they were not successful in persuading the Roosevelt Administration to adopt their proposal.

I was astonished to learn that Nobel Laureate Milton Friedman had long been an advocate of monetary reform. He had been associated in my mind with two theories, monetarism and a "natural rate" of unemployment, which, in their application to the real economy, I consider to be the two most unfortunate ideas to come on the economic stage since the Great Depression. It was with surprise and pleasure, then, that I found his name amongst the handful of pioneers who advocated an end to the fractional reserve system of banking and the substitution of a 100 percent reserve system.

First in an article entitled "A Monetary and Fiscal Framework for Economic Stability" published in the *American Economic Review*, in 1948,[7] and later in *A Program for Monetary Stability*, published in 1959,[8] Friedman makes the case for fundamental change. In the book he wrote: "As a student of Henry Simons and Lloyd Mints, I am naturally inclined to take the fractional reserve character of our commercial banking system as the focal point in a discussion of banking reform. I shall follow them also in recommending that the present system be replaced by one in which 100% reserves are required."[9]

I was even more surprised to learn that the economist whose work had influenced me the most at university, Irving Fisher, had also recommended a 100% reserve system of banking. It was his theory of money which first convinced me that recessions and depressions were monetary phenomena and, by extension, totally unnecessary. Not until the winter of 1993 did I become aware of his *100% Money*[10] and took the opportunity to read it. A man whose advice, had it been taken, would have helped us escape the worst ravages of the Great Depression, Fisher deserves a place high on the list of the great economists of all time.

Of course the idea of substituting government-created money for bank-created money was not original with these men despite the A+ they deserve for recognizing the merit of the concept. As we saw in Chapter 2, the American colonies had conducted experiments with government-created money as an alternative to borrowing from British banks. In Pennsylvania, for example, within a few years after that colony began to put paper money into circulation, with mortgaged real estate as security, a remarkable revival of its economy took place. It was reported that in Philadelphia in 1726, twice the number of ships were built as in any year previously.[11]

LINCOLN AND GOVERNMENT-CREATED MONEY

Although Abraham Lincoln was not a proponent of government-created money, he certainly recognized its usefulness in time of emergency. In his December 1862 message to Congress, Lincoln made the following reference to greenbacks: "The suspension of specie payments by banks soon after the commencement of your last session, made large issues of United States Notes [greenbacks] unavoidable. In no other way could the payment of the troops, and the satisfaction of other just demands, be so economically or so well provided for. The judicious legislation of Congress, securing the receivability of these notes for loans and internal duties, and making them a legal tender for other debts, has made them a universal currency; and has satisfied, partially, at least, and for the time, thereby to the people immense sums in discounts and exchanges."[12]

There was some Congressional support for adopting the system on a permanent basis. Representative Thaddeus Stevens, first elected to Congress as a Whig and later as a Republican, in speaking during the spirited debates over the first of the *Legal Tender Acts*, prior to the enactment of the legislation authorizing the printing of greenbacks,[13] said: "The government and not the banks should have the profit from creating a medium of exchange."[14] Another booster was Alexander Campbell, a mining engineer and entrepreneur, elected to Congress from Illinois in 1874 for a single term on a Democrat-Independent ticket. In *The True Greenback* he wrote: "The war has resulted in the complete overthrow and utter extinction of chattel slavery on this continent, but it has not destroyed the principle of oppression and wrong. The old pro-slaver serpent, beaten in the South, crawled up North and put on anti-slavery clothes and established his headquarters in Wall Street where ... he now, through bank monopolies and non-taxed bonds, rules the nation more despotically than under the old regime ... I assert, ... that an investment of a million dollars under the *National Banking Law*, or in non-taxed government securities, will yield a larger net income to its owner than a like amount invested in land and slaves employed in raising cotton and sugar did in the South in the palmiest days of the oligarchy."[15]

It was the bankers' view which carried the day, however. In March 1865, President Lincoln appointed a banker, Hugh McCulloch, secretary of the treasury. In a speech at Ft. Wayne, Indiana, in 1868, McCulloch said: "I look upon an irredeemable paper currency as an evil ... Gold and silver are the only true measures of value. I have myself no more doubt that these metals were prepared by the Almighty for this very purpose."[16]

Of course McCulloch's view of the Almighty did not end the controversy. Farmers, in particular, kept it alive. As grain prices fluctuated precariously, they became increasingly infuriated at what they considered to be usurious interest rates demanded by the banks, and government largesse toward the railroads. "The government had given four western railroads as much land as Ohio, Indiana, Michigan, and Wisconsin together, in addition to millions of dollars in loans or outright subsidies."[17] The farmers' acute unhappiness led to a kind of populism which embraced both the nationalization of money-creation and of the railroads. The platform of the People's Party of America in 1892, for example, called for "a national currency, safe, sound, and flexible, issued by the General Government only, a full legal tender for all debts, public and private, and this without the use of banking corporations ... the government to own and operate the railroads in the interest of the people."[18] Despite the valiant efforts of the dissenters, the bankers' orthodoxy prevailed.

CANADA AND SOCIAL CREDIT

Canadian opinion, as is often the case, paralleled that south of the border. Western farmers nursed the same two pet hates – the banks and the railroads. The boiling point came during the Great Depression when western unrest spawned new populist political parties including one called Social Credit, based primarily on the concept of monetary reform. It began as a provincial party which formed a government in Alberta, in 1935, where it tried to put its beliefs into practice. The Supreme Court of

Canada ruled the attempt unconstitutional because money and banking were the exclusive responsibility of the federal government.

Undeterred, the Social Crediters formed a federal party and elected a strong block of MPs who were already in Ottawa when I became a neophyte member in 1949. Their leader was Solon E. Low, an articulate Albertan backed by others including Victor Quelch, MP for Acadia, probably the most respected of the theorists, and John Blackmore, a Mormon priest who hammered away at the subject so consistently that there was a time when I could have repeated his remarks almost verbatim from memory.

The substance of their concern can be summed up in two brief quotes. The first from John Blackmore, "What Social Crediters have advocated is to create enough money, and to put it into circulation in the right places, to enable the purchasing power of the people to equal the amount of goods on sale in the market."[19] The second, as expressed by a subsequent leader of the party, Robert Thompson, is the one that kept ringing in my ears: "Our aim is to make financially possible what is physically possible."[20] In effect Thompson was proposing a marriage of the physical and paper economies, the best common sense I have heard from the leader of any political party at any time, anywhere.

The Social Credit party had been inspired, at least in part, by the writings of Major C.H. Douglas, a British engineer who, like a lot of ordinary people, gifted with a certain amount of common sense, had observed the periodic shortage of purchasing power in the British economy. To explain his position, Major Douglas employed his celebrated "A + B" theorem, in which he divided all costs of production into two categories. The "A" costs included all payments that producers (factories) made to individuals, such as wages, salaries and dividends, the "B" costs included all payments made to organizations for such things as raw materials, machinery, maintenance of plant, bank charges, etc.

The theorem was an abstraction and consequently ripped to shreds by the classical economists. Some of the things that Douglas identified, however, were perfectly valid. The periodic shortage of purchasing power, for example, would later be acknowledged by Keynes. In this respect both men questioned the validity of Say's law which had been such an impediment to the development of economic thought. Say's law was incorrect when it suggested that all production creates an equal and opposite demand. It obviously hadn't, and to pretend otherwise was a stumbling block of monumental proportions. A fundamental difference in principle between Douglas and Keynes, who lumped the engineer in with Marx as "underworld figures,"[21] was in their method of filling the purchasing gap. Douglas would use government-created money, while Keynes, as I indicated earlier, would have governments borrow their way to prosperity in the belief that eventually equilibrium would be restored and the extra debt would be repaid.

THE SOVEREIGNTY PROPOSAL

A more comprehensive suggestion was put forward in the United States by Kenneth Bohnsack. For several years he proposed that the United States Treasury be directed to create money and lend it, interest free, to junior tax-supported bodies for voter-approved capital projects. It was called the "Sovereignty Proposal." Perhaps it isn't too surprising that the idea was much more favorably received by the intended recipients than by those who would be charged with the implementation. I am advised that 1,828 tax-supported bodies endorsed the plan, as well as the U.S. Conference of Mayors representing 1,050 cities of 30,000 or more, where 80 million Americans reside; also the Bankers Association of Illinois, representing some 500 small banks, in addition to the House and Senate of Michigan.[22] Still the Sovereignty Proposal had many hurdles to overcome and never was accepted in mainstream economics.

A MIGHTY MOUNTAIN TO CLIMB

The absolute necessity of government-created money has been so well established by so many people over such a long period of time that in my opinion the case is iron-clad. There is no contest! The problem has been that reformers are their own worst enemies. There are almost as many different solutions as there are reformers. Some of their claims are exaggerated and many of their plans do not qualify as workable. They don't meet the test of common sense.

For example, a tabloid that arrived in my mail in July, 1994, proclaimed in respect of the Bank of Canada creation of debt-free money: "This will mean the end of debts, taxes, unemployment, bankruptcies, crises, and wars!"[23] The claim was so ridiculous that it was dismissed as fantasy. Regrettably the grain of truth was drowned in a sea of hyperbole, and the whole tract was destined for the paper recycling bin.

Another impediment was the proposal that reserves against deposits should be set at 100 percent. In Irving Fisher's *100% Money*, for example, he proposed the establishment of a "Currency Commission" which would buy bank assets for cash to the point where every commercial bank would have a cash reserve equal to 100% of its checking deposits – a state it would be required to maintain. As the banks would lose a large part of their interest-bearing assets they would be required to recover the lost income through service charges to their depositors.[24] Little wonder, then, that although Fisher managed to find two prominent bankers willing to support the idea the majority were strongly opposed.

Milton Friedman, well aware of the necessity to neutralize the bankers' objections, proposed paying interest on the 100% reserves. In *A Program For Monetary Stability* he said the following: "I shall depart from the original 'Chicago Plan of Banking Reform' in only one respect, though one that I think is of great importance. I shall urge that interest be paid on the 100% reserves. This step will both improve the economic results yielded by the 100% reserve system, and also, as a necessary consequence, render the system less subject to the difficulties of avoidance that were the bug-a-boo of the earlier proposals."[25] One of the serious problems, however, was what the rate of interest should be. "This problem of how to set the rate of interest is another issue that I feel most uncertain about and that requires more attention than I have given to it."[26] This is a concern I share and especially when I know how difficult it would be to ensure objectivity when banks are such generous supporters of the political system.

I could never support a proposal for 100% money because it defies all the tests of common sense, and practicality. Any attempt to implement such a solution would create both wild inflation and total chaos. There is no need for such extreme measures. After spending a lifetime studying and debating the alternatives I believe that my colleagues and I have developed the best solution of the many available to meet the many criteria of justice, fairness, and workability that I will propose in a later chapter.

Meanwhile I will share a little more about the pitfalls and triumphs of climbing the Monetary Mountain.

CHAPTER FIVE

THE LONG, LONG ROAD TO DISCOVERY

"All great truths begin as blasphemies."
– George Bernard Shaw

It was the conventional wisdom in 1948 that we would suffer another Depression in 1950 that motivated me to try to get elected to the Canadian House of Commons in June 1949 at the tender age of 25. I was convinced that neither recessions nor Depressions were necessary. They were monetary phenomena and I felt morally bound to try to do something about the one my economics professors had predicted.

I recruited a few friends to help me and in a few short weeks, beginning in the middle of the campaign, we managed to pull off a victory in a riding that was considered to be "impossible." It was a minor miracle if there ever was one. So off I went to Ottawa where I soon learned the first lesson of politics. Just because you and your family have your picture on the front page of the second section of the Toronto Star, Canada's largest circulation newspaper, doesn't mean that you are a somebody when you get to Ottawa.

Backbenchers, as neophyte Members of Parliament are called, don't have significant influence on any kind of policy, and certainly not monetary policy. As fate would dictate, it didn't matter. There was no Depression in 1950 because the Korean War began and governments that can't find enough money in peacetime are quite willing to borrow the funds necessary to wage a successful war.

By the time that the Korean Armistice occurred the money supply was sufficient to finance a prosperous economy for almost two decades. The division of income between government, capital and labor seemed acceptable to all, and we enjoyed what became fondly remembered as the Fifteen Golden Years.

When I first arrived in Ottawa Keynesian economics reigned supreme. Robert Bryce, the Clerk of the Privy Council and principal advisor to the prime minister, was a staunch supporter of Keynes. The same was true of the senior people in the Finance Department. It would be fair to say that the vast majority of members of the "in group" of the permanent staff were loyal followers of the English guru. So, I am told, was U.S. President Richard Nixon.

About two decades later a new wave began to appear on the horizon. It was labeled Monetarism, and sometimes Friedmanism, although that was the professor's second choice. For a long time he had been a supporter of 100% cash reserves. As late as 1983 in a footnote reply to a letter from William F. Hixson, Friedman wrote "As good a reform as ever, unfortunately with as little prospect of adoption as ever. I keep mentioning it but feel that tilting at windmills is not an effective way to spend my time."[1] If he had been content to let it go at that, the Nobel laureate would have earned a place among the forward-looking thinkers on a fundamentally important issue.

In a 1986 letter to Professor John H. Hotson, in reply to one on the subject of reserves and government-created money, he wrote: "In my opinion, either extreme is acceptable. I have not given up advocacy of one-hundred percent reserves. I would prefer one-hundred percent reserves to the alternative I set forth. However, I believe that getting the government out of the business altogether, or zero percent reserves, also makes sense. The virtue of either one is that it eliminates government meddling in the lending and investing activities of the financial markets. When I wrote in 1948, we were already halfway toward one-hundred percent reserves because so large a fraction of the assets of the banks consisted of either government bonds or high-powered money. One-hundred percent reserves at that time did not look impossible of achievement. We have moved so far since then that I am very skeptical indeed that there is any political possibility of achieving one-hundred percent reserves. That does not mean that it is not desirable."[2]

Professor Friedman goes on to say that the sole reason he stressed the zero percent reserves was "because it seemed to me at least to be within the imaginable range of political feasibility."[3] He was correct on that point as three countries, including Canada, were pioneers in adopting the policy. But that doesn't mean it makes sense. One could argue that it is one of the worst ideas to emerge from the academy in the history of economics. What Friedman was suggesting was a system based almost exclusively on debt, which is the inverted pyramid that Irving Fisher found so worrisome. It is the same inverted pyramid, grotesquely exaggerated in recent debates, which makes the present system inherently unstable. One has to be skeptical of a theory based on political expediency rather than common sense.

A zero reserve system, with its incredible leverage, is not only inherently unstable, but it will ultimately implode with a world-shattering crash. A 100% reserve system is not really feasible either, due to the size and importance of the banking industry and its need to have some revenues in addition to the growing list of service charges. So it seems that a pragmatic, middle of the road course should be the order of the day – a solution that will reduce leverage to a sound level, reverse the ratio of debt to GDP, and still keep the banks in business.

THE COMMITTEE ON MONETARY & ECONOMIC REFORM (COMER)

I can't remember exactly when it was, but at some point I was introduced to the organization known as The Committee on Monetary and Economic Reform (COMER). It was founded by Professor John Hotson who taught Economics at the University of Waterloo, Ontario, in concert with William Krehm, musician, music critic, political radical, iconoclast and businessman who amassed a fair-sized fortune in real estate. Together, with Krehm picking up the tab, they established a monthly news bulletin titled COMER. The bond between the two men, and the many other men and women who were attracted to them, was a common belief that federal governments should create money for their own needs.

When I first met Hotson we bonded at once because we were of like mind. He had the advantage of a better grasp of the technical details so he became a kind of tutor. He wanted me to join COMER but understood when I explained why that was impossible while I was still in active politics. The press were merciless in their treatment of any member of parliament who admitted any interest in what they scathingly described as "funny money." I was aware that one member of the press gallery, the influential Charlie Lynch who disliked me intensely for unifying the three armed forces, would have gleefully ripped the political skin right off my back in his widely-read column.

Hotson understood the political risk so we kept our relationship private. It became sufficiently close that when John died his wife advised me that I should have my choice of any or all of the books in his personal library. I took as many as my already overloaded book shelves could accommodate.

When my twenty-two and a half years as a member of parliament end-ed in 1974, I felt free to join COMER and collaborate freely with its many talented members. I got to know Bill Krehm on a first name basis and my appreciation of his incredible life kept growing. Two very active members of COMER, Ann Emmett and Jerry Ackerman, ran as candidates for my ill-fated Canadian Action Party.

Later still I made inquiries about finding a bona fide economist who I could work with in preparing a proposal for our government. I had ended the equivalent of a lifetime in partisan politics in the Spring of 2004 when I had resigned as leader of the Canadian Action Party. Since then I have had no further allegiance to any political party because the several issues that I consider critically important are not partisan issues. They are people is-sues, affecting the whole of humankind. So I don't care which party "bites the bullet" as the saying goes. I only hope and pray that some party will.

It wasn't too long before I got a response to my inquiry, the president of the Kingston, Ontario Branch of COMER, Richard Priestman, phoned to say that they had a real economist. His name was Keith Wilde, would I like to meet him? Would I? You bet I would! So a meeting was arranged and I drove to Kingston to have lunch with this possible recruit. There are a few economists who are believers, but the ones who will stick their necks out and risk ridicule are very rare!

Richard introduced me to Keith who had worked for the Bank of Can-ada briefly, and for the federal government for the remainder of his career. It didn't take long to establish that our views were very similar and that we were both monetary reformers who believed that government-creat-ed money was not only possible, but absolutely essential. After coffee he summed up the discussion by saying: "At last, a politician who 'gets it'!" I had the decency, or it may have been just common sense, not to reply: "At last, an economist who 'gets it'!"

Keith and I worked together for a long time until he became too ill to continue. My files of our correspondence are the most voluminous of any in my several filing cabinets. He was a wonderful friend and partner in a common quest. Our only difference was in a definition. He claimed that all money was debt, and I insisted that wasn't necessarily so. Lincoln's Greenbacks were debt free. Later cash money issued by the United States of America were debt free. They simply say "This note is legal tender for all debts public and private."

United States cash issued by the Federal Reserve is similarly marked "This note is legal tender for all debts public and private." Canadian Bank of Canada notes don't say anything but are similarly legal tender for all debts public and private, although in some disgusting cases they are not accepted as such. My final example was coins. I have a small handful of silver and gold coins. They are mine, and not indebted to anyone in any way.

Keith would have been correct if he had said that most money is debt. All bank-created money (BCM) is debt, and all bank deposits are debt. They are "I owe you's" from the bank to its customers and comprise about 97 percent of the "money" supply. It isn't real money, however, it is just virtual money – computer entries, to be exact. This fact is the reason for the chronic instability of the banking system. In any event Keith and I decided not to get hung up on a definition and got on with the creation of a plan to insert significant amounts of government-created money (GCM) into the system.

We knew that our proposal would work because I had spent quite a lot of money on econometric simulation. The company I used was Informetrica Limited., whose president Mike McCracken was widely respected by business and the press because it had acquired state of the art software in economic projection. Mike assigned his vice-president, Carl Sonnen, to be in charge of my file. I will never forget the day Carl phoned and left a message that read "The results are so good they are scary."

When I got back to the office and saw the message I was ecstatic, but not really too surprised because the computer had just converted common sense into numbers. Informetrica was so impressed that they agreed to a joint press conference, something they had never done before. Unfortunately we were "bumped" by a couple of other items that seemed much less significant to us, and there were only three or four good reporters, including the one for the Canadian Press News Agency, who were still in the room to hear our good news story. They were writing furiously, and I expected that we would get good coverage.

It was Easter weekend so I scanned the Friday newspapers, and again those that published on Saturday. I checked the radio and television news reports thoroughly but there was not a word reported. Not one word! After years of study and the expenditure of significant funds to prove the theory the public was left totally in the dark. I was devastated. It was just like being dead.

I bounce back quickly however, so when Keith arrived on the scene the two of us, in collaboration with a few other COMER stalwarts, began to work on a comprehensive proposal to present to the government of Canada. We got along famously and found that our experience was complementary. After months of hard slugging we finally came up with an agreed document called A Social Contract Between the Government and People of Canada. It was endorsed by 40 monetary reformers and sent to Finance Minister James Flaherty, with copies to the leaders of the three opposition parties.

A SOCIAL CONTRACT BETWEEN THE GOVERNMENT AND PEOPLE OF CANADA

In view of the fact that our present banking and financial system is unstable and unsustainable, we, the undersigned, on behalf of all Canadians, demand that the federal government use its constitutional power over all matters pertaining to money and banking by forthwith taking the following action to benefit all Canadians:

1. The government of Canada should print fifteen non-transferable, non-convertible, non-redeemable $10 billion nominal value Canada share certificates.

2. Simultaneously, the Justice Department should be asked for a legal opinion as to whether the share certificates qualify as collateral under the Bank of Canada Act. If not, legislation should be introduced to amend the Act to specify their eligibility.

3. The government should then present the share certificates to the Bank of Canada that would forthwith book the certificates as assets against the liability of the cash created, and deposit $150 billion in the government's bank accounts. The federal government should immediately transfer $75 billion to the various provinces and territories in amounts proportional to their population, with the understanding that they would help the municipalities, as appropriate, so that there would be no need to cut back on essential services, or to sell valuable assets.

4. Amend the Bank Act to reverse the 1991 amendments that eliminated the requirement for the Canadian chartered banks to maintain cash reserves against their deposits, and provide the Minister of Finance, or someone acting on his or her behalf, the power to set the level of cash reserves for banks and other deposit-taking institutions up to a maximum of 34%, provided the increase is not less than 5% per annum until the new 34% base has been established in 7 years. This will ensure that there will be no inflation resulting from the government-created money.

5. The government should repeat the action prescribed in Sections 1 and 3 every year for 7 years or until bank cash reserves reach 34% of their total assets.

6. Once the transition has been made the Governor of the central bank shall, each year, estimate the amount of increase in the money stock required to keep the economy growing at its optimum with the number of job openings being roughly equal to the number of job seekers. He/she shall then acquire, on a predetermined schedule, shares from the federal government in exchange for cash up to 34% of that amount.

7. In the event of a disagreement between the Governor and the Minister of Finance in respect to the amount by which the money supply should be increased, or the rate of interest to be charged by the bank for overnight lending, the view of the Minister shall prevail. In any such case, however, a direction from the Minister shall be in writing and made public forthwith. This procedure is consistent with the principles of democracy, and should eliminate future cases of monetary and fiscal policies being at odds rather than working in harmony.

This is the basic formula that I will be recommending for general application later in the book. I will also explain why I consider it to be the best option of the several alternatives being proposed by other equally dedicated monetary reformers.

The Social Contract is a streamlined and modernized version of the system that was used in Canada from 1949 to 1974 with such amazingly good results. I refer to it as the Canadian Precedent in a number of documents and in my book titled The Money Mafia, from which an excerpt is copied here.

THE CANADIAN PRECEDENT

In 1938 there were no job openings in Canada – none! Then, in 1939, World War II began and it wasn't long until everyone was either in the armed forces, or working in factories to build the tanks, trucks, airplanes and ships required to support a really magnificent war effort. Unemployment dropped to an historic low of one percent.

You may wonder where the Canadian government got the money to initiate this unprecedented economic miracle. The answer is that the Bank of Canada printed it. The Bank bought government of Canada bonds and paid for them with newly minted cash. The government paid the Bank interest on the bonds which then, because the government owned 100% of the Bank shares, was returned as dividends, with only the cost of administration deducted. In effect, it was near zero cost money that produced such wondrous results.

The newly created money that the government spent into circulation wound up in the private banks where it became what the economists called "high-powered money". High-powered money was really "legal tender" money or "real money" that the banks could use as "cash reserves" which the law allowed them to leverage into bank loans equal to 12½ times their reserves. So if $10 million of what was literally government-created money was ultimately deposited in one of the commercial banks, the banking system was able to create an additional $125 million in book-entry or "virtual" money.

The commercial banks were able to lend this money to help businesses build factories, develop essential products, buy "War Bonds," etc. These large infusions of first government-created cash, followed by bank-created credit, made it possible for Canada to be transformed in a few short years from a largely agricultural and resource-based economy into a significant mixed economy that included a strong manufacturing, industrial and scientific base.

What made this all financially possible was a sharing of the money-creation function between government and the commercial banks. That enabled Canada not only to play a larger-than-life role in the war effort, but also to extend the miracle into the post-war years.

Government-created money played a key role in many of our infrastructure projects like the great St. Lawrence Seaway development, the Trans-Canada highway, new airport terminals and port facilities. It also enabled the federal government to assist the provinces and municipalities with many of their major public works ranging from bridges to sewage-disposal systems.

Another marvellous benefit that government-created money helped make possible was the establishment of a social security network to help citizens in times of distress. Some of us who had lived through the Great Depression of the 1930s were determined that never again would someone lose their home, farm or life savings due to a serious illness of one of the members of the family. Nor would someone be left destitute because he or she was unemployed. All of these accomplishments were achieved without incurring any significant debt.

This system of money-creation sharing between the government and private banks worked splendidly for 35 years until 1974, when the Bank of Canada unilaterally changed the rules. As far as I know – and I and others have spent many hours of research without finding any evidence that would refute it – this was done without either advising or obtaining the consent of the Canadian government that owns 100% of the shares on behalf of the Canadian taxpayers.

The Governor of the Bank of Canada simply put it into effect and didn't tell the Canadian people until September 1975 in a speech in Western Canada.[4] Meanwhile he was in discussions with ten other Central Bank Governors concerning the establishment of the Basel Committee that became known as the Committee on Banking Regulations and Supervisory Practices at the end of 1974.

There was no mention that we were leaping into the arms of The Bank for International Settlements (BIS), with its plan to manage the World economy. Its policy of not allowing central banks to provide cheap money to their governments was like a knock-out blow in boxing, from which we have never recovered.

A phone call from my friend Ellen Hodgson Brown really blew my mind. "Paul", she said, "did you know that Canadians have paid a trillion dollars in interest, and none of it was necessary?" I have the highest regard for Ellen but I was incredulous. So I asked the research department of our Parliamentary Library to check. The answer came back that from fiscal 1974/1975, to fiscal 2010/2011, Canadian taxpayers had paid one trillion, one hundred million dollars in interest on federal debt alone. Almost all of it unnecessary. Just imagine what that much money could have accomplished if it had been spent for useful pursuits! Obviously an up-to-date figure would be far greater. Our American cousins fared even worse.

So what about this BIS beast that allegedly runs the world? Most of my friends have never heard of it. So the next chapter, The Bank for International Settlements, has been copied verbatim from my book The Money Mafia, A World in Crisis.[5] It is not a pretty picture.

CHAPTER SIX

THE BANK FOR INTERNATIONAL SETTLEMENTS

"To be frank, I have no use for politicians.
They lack the judgment of central bankers."
– Fritz Leutwiler, BIS president and chairman
of the board, 1982-1984[1]

You might wonder why I am dedicating a whole chapter to a bank that most of my friends have never heard of. The Fed and the IMF are household words, but the BIS? What is it? It just happens to be one of the most influential and powerful non-governmental institutions of the 20th century, and it played a key role in the formation of the European monetary union.

The Bank for International Settlements (BIS) was established on May 17, 1930 through an intergovernmental agreement by Germany, Belgium, France, Great Britain and Northern Ireland, Italy, Japan, the United States and Switzerland.[2,3] Its original purpose was to facilitate the payment of reparations imposed on Germany by the Treaty of Versailles after World War I.[4]

The need to establish a dedicated institution for this purpose was recommended by a committee headed by American Owen D. Young, that had been set up to reduce the extent of reparations when it became obvious that Germany could not meet the annual payments established earlier. The Young Plan reduced further payments to 112 billion Gold Marks from the previous level of 269 billion.

I had just written a few paragraphs beyond this point when my Guardian Angel came to the rescue. A friend that I hadn't heard from for a long time sent me an e-mail to an old address where it was just discovered by accident.

He had just read a new book entitled *Tower of Basel: The Shadowy History of the Secret Bank that Runs the World*, by Adam Lebor. My friend was aware of my lifelong interest in money and banking, and thought I might be interested in reading it. That was an understatement. I devoured every word of its 272 meticulously researched pages that proved, beyond doubt, my preconceived prejudice.

I had planned to mention the BIS connection to the Nazis, and also its incredible secrecy and lack of transparency to the point that neither presidents, prime ministers nor ministers of finance can attend its meetings, leading me to conclude that the BIS should go the way of all flesh. Adam Lebor's book drove the final nail in the coffin.

I return now, to where I left off, inspired by Lebor's insights. Whereas the alleged reason for the new bank was to manage Germany's war reparations, the real purpose of the BIS was detailed in its statutes: to "Promote the cooperation of central banks and to provide additional facilities for international financial operations." It was the culmination of the central bankers' decades-old dream which was to have their own bank – powerful, independent, and free from interfering politicians and nosy reporters. Most felicitous of all, the BIS was self-financing and would be in perpetuity. This advantage was facilitated, at least in part, by its success in negotiating tax-exempt status from the government of Switzerland. Its clients were its own founders and shareholders – the central banks of the world.[5]

"During the 1930s, the BIS was the central meeting place for a cabal of central bankers, dominated by Norman [Montagu Norman, Governor of the Bank of England] and Schacht [Hjalmar Schacht, president of the Reichsbank]. This group helped rebuild Germany. The *New York Times* described Schacht, widely acknowledged as the genius behind the resurgent German economy, as 'The Iron-Willed Pilot of Nazi Finance.'[6] During the war, the BIS became a de-facto arm of the Reichsbank, accepting looted Nazi gold and carrying out foreign exchange deals for Nazi Germany."[7]

In the pre-war period, there was solid collaboration between American and German industrialists. IG Farben, the octopus corporation, operated in the U.S. as General Aniline and Film (GAF). GAF's founding board members included Walter Teagle, president of Standard Oil; Edsel Ford, the president of Ford Motors; Charles E. Mitchell, chairman of National City Bank; and Paul Warburg, of the banking dynasty. GAF's most important partner was Standard Oil, that was also on excellent terms with the BIS.

The BIS's aid to Germany was constant. It accepted Germany's writeoff of its pre-war reparation debt with barely a whimper. It accepted the Nazi annexation of Austria as routine and facilitated the transfer of both the Austrian National Bank's gold reserves and their 4,000 BIS shares to the Reichsbank. The takeover of the Sudetenland, the border province that Czechoslovakia had been forced to cede to the Nazis in September 1938, while much more complicated due to the Czechoslovaks' banks 143 branches in the province, presented no great problem to the BIS.

Another interesting point that Lebor mentions in his book is the benefit of American technology bestowed on the German war machine.

"War had brought enormous profits to the American car industry. Opel, General Motors' German division, produced the 'Blitz' truck on which the Wehrmacht invaded Poland. Ford's German subsidiary produced almost half of all the two- and three-ton trucks in Nazi Germany. There is a strong argument that without General Motors' and Ford's German subsidiaries, the Nazis would not have been able to wage war.[8] Hitler was certainly an enthusiastic supporter of the American motor industry's methods of mass production. He even kept a portrait of Henry Ford by his desk."[9]

While the pre-war and wartime activities of the various players are worrisome enough, a careful reading of what happened after the Nazis realized they were going to lose the war, and the collusion of some of the allied forces, leads to the unhappy conclusion that what is past might just be prologue. It is a suspicion that one must take seriously.

The Allies were persuaded not to bomb the IG Farben empire and reduce it to dust as they could have done. The logic was to facilitate a fast post-war recovery of Germany's industrial base as a bulwark against the Soviet Union. Plans were already underway for a post-war united Europe that would prevent Germany from ever again launching a war that would require American intervention. So, for the U.S., integration leading to some kind of political union was not an option, it was essential.

Meanwhile the Germans were exporting capital in order to flee when the war was over. Harry Dexter White, an economist, told a meeting of Treasury officials in July 1944, during the Bretton Woods conference, that Nazi leaders were preparing to flee the country or have their property confiscated. "They bought estates and industries and corporations, and there is evidence that the German corporations have been buying into South American corporations in expectation of being able to re-establish themselves there after the war."[10] The cloaking operation was extremely complex, White continued. "They are working through first, second and third fronts, so it is pretty hard to trace it without having all the data available." The Treasury officials also discussed the BIS at the same meeting, noting that out of twenty-one board members and senior officials, sixteen were "representatives of countries that are either now our enemies, or are occupied," including Walther Funk and Hermann Schmitz.[11]

"As the Allies advanced on Germany, the Nazis stepped up their plans for the post-war era. On August 10, 1944, an elite group of industrialists gathered at the Maison Rouge Hotel in Strasbourg, including representatives of Krupp, Messerschmitt, Volkswagen, and officials from several ministries. Also in attendance was a French spy, whose report reached the headquarters of the Allied invasion force, from where it was forwarded to the State Department and the Treasury. The account of the meeting is known as the Red House Report.

"Germany had lost the war, the Nazi industrialists agreed, but the struggle would continue along new lines. *The Fourth Reich would be a financial, rather than a military imperium.* The industrialists were to plan for a 'post-war commercial campaign.' They should make 'contacts and alliances' with foreign firms but ensure this was done without 'attracting any suspicion.' Large sums would have to be borrowed from foreign countries. Just as in the pre-war era, the U.S. connection and links to chemical firms, such as the American Chemical Foundation, were essential to expanding German interests. The Zeiss lens company, the Leica camera firm, and the Hamburg-American line had been 'especially effective in protecting German interests abroad.' The firms' New York addresses were passed around the world.

"A smaller group attended a second, select meeting. There the industrialists were instructed to 'prepare themselves to finance the Nazi party, which would be forced to go underground.' The prohibition against exporting capital had been lifted, and the government would help the industrialists to send as much money to neutral countries as possible, through two Swiss banks. The Nazi party recognized that after the defeat, its best-known leaders would be 'condemned as war criminals,' the intelligence report concluded. However, the party and the industrialists were cooperating in placing the most important figures in positions at German factories as research or technical experts."[12]

"Emil Puhl [vice-president of Germany's Reichsbank] discussed the Nazi leadership's post-war strategy with [Thomas] McKittrick at the BIS in March 1945, during the last few weeks of the war. The information he passed to McKittrick echoes that included in the Red House Report and Harry Dexter White's discussion at Bretton Woods. Military defeat was merely a temporary setback. The Nazis were fanatics and would never give up their ideals, Puhl explained. Instead, they would go underground.

McKittrick immediately informed Allen Dulles of the conversation. Dulles sent the information on to London, Paris, and Washington on March 21, 1945. His telegram noted that Puhl had 'just arrived' in Basel:"[13]

"He said that the jig was up but that Nazis had made careful plans to go underground, that every essential figure had his designated place, that Nazism would not end with military defeat as Hitler and his fanatical followers would no more change their philosophy than would Socrates or Mohammed, that these men were just as convinced of their cause as ever and carried a great body of people with them. He emphasized that Nazism was like a religion, not merely a political regime."[14]

It is not surprising, given its role in providing friendly assistance to Germany both during its period of ascendance during the 1930s and then during the war years under the guise of financial neutrality, that there was a strong demand for abolition of the BIS. Henry Morgenthau, U.S. Secretary of the Treasury and Harry White both wanted it abolished. On July 10, 1944, they seemed about to get their wish. Wilhelm Keilhau, of the Norwegian delegation at Bretton Woods introduced a motion to liquidate the BIS.

No one spoke publicly in defense of the BIS. But behind the scenes its defenders – sections of the State Department, Wall Street, the Bank of England, the British Treasury, and Foreign Office – went into action. There was a bitter battle between those who wanted to see the German war machine completely dismantled after the war and those who envisaged a penitent giant re-emerging from the ashes as key players in a new united Europe.

"Harry White saw the BIS clearest. The bank's emphasis on its supposed neutrality was an alibi for its future role in reconstructing Europe, he argued:

"They hope to be a moderating influence in the treatment of Germany during the peace conference. That is why Germany has treated it with the greatest of care. She has permitted her to pay dividends; she has let the people in BIS come and go across enemy territory; she has been extremely careful and well-disposed to the BIS, because she nursed that baby along in the hope that that would be a useful agency that would protect her interests beyond that of any other institution around the peace table would."[15]

The Germans were not the only ones who recognized the future usefulness of the BIS. The same was true of powerful banking interests in the City of London and on Wall Street. These top banking barons are the ones who pull the strings to make presidents and prime ministers dance. The bankers must have believed that they could use the BIS to screen the real centers of power in the Western World. If so, their prescience was remarkable because that is exactly how the real world has evolved.

The close connection between the banking industry and the big transnational industries is another area where close collaboration was to become the dominant factor. So the lines between justice for horrendous crimes and geo-political interests became hopelessly blurred.

"In July 1945 the U.S. occupation authorities asked Dulles to furnish a list of Germans 'eligible on the basis of ability and political record for posts in a reconstituted German administration.' The first set of lists was quickly submitted. But by autumn, Dulles, now running the OSS station in Berlin, had more detailed information about suitable German bankers. Much of this would have come from McKittrick.

"In September 1945 Dulles submitted his new white list. It was divided into two categories: A and B. On the A list were three names judged suitable for 'higher posts in a ministry.' The B list contained five names that were suggested for 'lesser posts such as Bureau head or division chief.'[16] Among the names in group A was that of Ernst Hülse, the former head of the BIS banking department. Hülse, said Dulles, enjoyed 'excellent connections with banking circles abroad,' had a Jewish wife, and was definitely anti-Nazi. Hülse was appointed to the Reichsbank in the British zone and was named president of the central bank for the federal state of Nordheim-Westfalen.

"The name on the B list was that of Karl Blessing, whom Dulles described as a 'prominent businessman and financial expert' with 'considerable experience in international trade.'"[17]

Dulles did not mention that Blessing had been arrested and imprisoned while the Allies considered whether to charge him with war crimes consistent with his record. Nor did he say that he had supported Blessing's release.

"The whitewashing of Blessing was not the exception, but the Rule. Declassified telegrams revealed that Dulles had long planned to rescue important German industrialists and scientists. In January 1945, Dulles wrote to William J. Casey, who was running operations inside Germany and who later served as CIA director in the 1980s:

"My project contemplates that in normal course of events and without any prior contact with us but merely to escape impending chaos, important German industrialists, scientists, etc., will desire to find some haven, preferably Switzerland. If Switzerland is closed to them, these men might possibly turn to

Russia as their only alternative…. Discreet preliminary conversations indicate some hope of securing Swiss cooperation."[18]

"Not everyone in Washington approved. The following month First Lady Eleanor Roosevelt wrote to her husband, 'Memo for the President. Allen Dulles who is in charge of Bill Donovan's outfit in Paris has been counsel, closely tied up with the Schroeder Bank. That is likely to be the representative of the underground Nazi interests after the war. There seems to be in Paris a great many people who are pretty close to the big business side!"[19]

"The president's wife was certainly well informed about the importance of the Schröder bank network, which reached from Germany to London and New York, and to the BIS via Kurt von Schröder. But by summer 1945, after the death of her husband, Mrs. Roosevelt's opinions counted for little in Washington."[20]

Pity! The die was cast. The vast majority of top Nazis had escaped trial and punishment. Many were appointed to important posts in their own country while others relocated to other countries in Europe and South America. The United States, thanks first to Operation Paperclip and then post-war immigration, became home to a very large contingent, many of whom were placed in positions of significant influence.

The BIS escaped the guillotine and, after a bit of a rough patch, emerged triumphant and flourishing. Its membership increased. Its influence became all pervasive. It played a significant role in the unification of Europe. Most important of all, just as the top bankers had hoped, it became a powerful vehicle for the transfer of power from democratic nation states to an unelected, unaccountable, bureaucratic institution acting on the private advice from the world's top bankers.

It has usurped the power of nation states to establish their own rules and reserve requirements for banks and used their puppet central bankers to advise their respective governments to accept BIS rules as normal in a new international world order. For this I can never forgive them.

Canada had a quite satisfactory system in place from 1939-1974 when the money creation function was shared between the federal government and the private banks. It worked well and gave us the best years of the 20th century. Then the BIS butted in and persuaded the Bank of Canada to abandon its shareholders, the Canadian people, and buy the notion that privately-owned banks were entitled to a de facto monopoly to manufacture money. But, tragically, all of it as debt that can never, ever, be repaid. Hence austerity and moribund economies operating well below their potential.

The BIS drew up a set of international rules called Basel I. These were not compulsory but were promoted as universally desirable. When the first shot proved to be less than perfect they were re-written as Basel II. The banks were still able to keep their slot-machine manufacturing capability where they put in a nickel and get a dollar back in return – plus interest, of course.

After the Wall Street meltdown of 2007-2008, from which the world suffered for more than a decade, it became obvious that BIS rules were inadequate to prevent such crimes against humanity. Consequently, the BIS scrambled to devise Basel III. I read through it recently and it still resembles Swiss cheese with holes big enough to drive a tank through. No wonder the bankers love the BIS.

To give the appearance of doing something new and helpful the BIS established an organization called the Financial Stability Board. Despite the advertising, and the gentle hand of Mark Carney, former governor of the Bank of Canada and then promoted to Governor of the Bank of England, it is still fraudulently labelled. It is still a Financial Instability Board in reality, despite the hype to the contrary.

THE BANK FOR INTERNATIONAL SETTLEMENTS IS HOPELESS!

In its annual report in June 2013, it said:

> Six years have passed since the eruption of the global financial crisis, yet robust, self-sustaining, well balanced growth still eludes the global economy… Central banks cannot do more without compounding the risks they have already created… [They must] encourage needed adjustments of ever-larger quantities of government securities… Delivering further extraordinary monetary stimulus is becoming increasingly perilous, as the balance between its benefits and costs is shifting. Monetary stimulus alone cannot provide the answer because the roots of the problem are not monetary. Hence, central banks must manage a return to their stabilization role, allowing others to do the hard but essential work of adjustment.

For "adjustment," read "structural adjustment" – imposing austerity measures on the people in order to balance budgets and pay down national debts. In plain English that means a kind of permanent recession that denies many millions of people the opportunity to find useful employment and the self respect of contributing to their own welfare. In my opinion this is not even worthy of discussion!

Even before reading Adam Lebor's book I was convinced that the BIS should be on the execution list. Its pre-war and post-war record is unacceptable to anyone who believes in democratic responsibility. Its addiction to privilege, fine dining, vintage wines and exemption from taxation provide exactly the wrong principles for a world seeking meaning and direction. Its elitist attitude is offensive to those who believe in equality of opportunity.

Most alarming of all, it aids and abets the robber barons and their Ponzi scheme which impoverishes much of the world and is undermining the very existence of Western civilization as we have known it. It has to be replaced by an institution that works for the people rather than against them. It won't be easy and probably can't be done until the Fed is nationalized and it, or its successor central Bank of the United States casts its ballot in favor of a new World Bank for International Settlements.

I would urge anyone who is genuinely concerned about the future of planet Earth to read the *Tower of Basel*, by Adam Lebor, and make up your own mind about the nature of the crisis upon which the future of the world depends.

CHAPTER SEVEN

MONETARISM IS MACHIAVELLIAN

"Zero cash reserves is the sweetest swindle ever concocted"
Paul Hellyer

We learned in the last chapter that the would-be masters of the world planned to use the financial system as heavy artillery in their war of conquest. So far they have succeeded brilliantly. Their "End Game" was confirmed by a former insider. According to Professor Carroll Quigley, Bill Clinton's mentor at Georgetown University, it has all been a part of a concerted plan by a clique of international financiers. He wrote in *Tragedy and Hope* in 1964:

> The powers of financial capitalism had another far-reaching aim, nothing less than to create a world system of financial control in private hands able to dominate the political system of each country and the economy of the world as a whole. This system was to be controlled in a feudalist fashion by the central banks of the world acting in concert, by secret agreements arrived at in frequent private meetings and conferences. The apex of the system was to be the Bank for International Settlements in Basel, Switzerland, a private bank owned and controlled by the world's central banks which were themselves private corporations.[1]

While the "End Game" has long been clear, the "Banksters," as some of my reformer friends have labelled them, needed some academic and market support as justification. Their luck held when Milton Friedman rode to the rescue. As I pointed out earlier, Friedman had been a supporter of the 100% reserve system favoured by his mentors from the original Chicago School of the 1930s even though he didn't know how to make it work. Someone would have to pay the banks interest on the reserves. But who and how much was still to be resolved. The government might have to get involved.

Although Friedman has not renounced his support for a 100% reserve system it was no longer on his priority list as indicated in a footnote reply to a 1983 letter from William F. Hixson. "As good a reform as ever," Friedman wrote, "… unfortunately with as little prospect of adoption as ever. I keep mentioning it but feel that tilting at windmills is not an effective way to spend my time."[2] If he had been content to let it go at that, the Nobel laureate would have earned a place among the forward-looking thinkers on a fundamentally important issue. But in subsequent writings he has recommended freezing the production of the government money and the adoption of zero percent reserves.

Not only did Dr. Friedman's flip-flop from 100% cash reserves to zero cash reserves produce disastrous results, his failure to fully appreciate that there was more than one kind of inflation was another fatal flaw in his analysis. He appeared to believe that our economies were genuine markets instead of increasingly rigid ones. Consequently, there was only one kind of inflation.

The theory of economics has no mathematical formula to quantify a phenomenon that is as much political and sociological as economic. A phenomenon, nonetheless, that has incalculable economic consequences. The impact from the unregulated power of monopolies, oligopolies and trade unions, even in cases where natural monopolies have their prices to consumers regulated, find that one of their principal costs is not. So wage increases, no matter how great, are just passed through to the consuming public.

I recall a former president of Bell Telephone of Canada – a monopoly at the time – vehemently insisting that big business was responsible enough to police its own labour settlements in a manner compatible with the public interest. Only weeks later his company signed a pace-setting agreement in order to avoid a strike. Naturally, Bell was allowed to pass the highly inflationary cost increases on to its subscribers without penalty. The magnitude of the negotiated inflationary settlement in this example became a benchmark for diverse service unions.

In practice, oligopolies have a profound influence on prices. I think it was John Stuart Mill who said that they don't meet to set prices, they just make their plans over tea. They then adjourn and presto, prices start to rise in concert over the course of a few days or weeks. I had some evidence of this years ago when I was raising money for a capital project of the Ottawa YMCA, I made an appointment with one of the presidents of a major Canadian bank. I asked for a commitment but he said he couldn't give me one that day. "We get together on these things, you know," he said, referring to the other big banks. "Yes, I know," I responded, "but I didn't think you would ever admit it."

To the extent that oligopolies have the collective market power to pass cost increases on to the consuming public, they are less responsible in policing their own settlements. Like big labour, big business puts its own perceived short-term interests first. Consequently, many contracts are signed that appear beneficial to business or labor or both but may be detrimental to the public interest.

Whether by monopolies, oligopolies or governments, it has been the approval of wage increases well in excess of average productivity that led inexorably to an ever higher-level of underlying inflation. Each additional increase, whether in response to higher oil prices, more expensive food, or just a desire to keep up with a new record settlement, gave the spiral another twist.

WAGES OUT OF JOINT WITH PRODUCTIVITY

I argued earlier in this book that in the late 1960's and 1970's the principal cause of inflation in Western industrialized economies was nominal wage increases being out-of-joint with productivity. Oil shocks and other price changes produced blips but the trend line was determined by the gap between nominal wages and real output.

Most economists recognized that there was a relationship between wages and prices. The President's Council of Economic Advisers was right on target in its 1981 report in saying: "... since payments to labor are estimated to account for almost two-thirds of total production costs, prices over the long term tend to move in conjunction with changes in labor unit costs."[3]

Precisely! In the longer term, prices move up at a rate that approximates the increase in wages and fringe benefits minus the increase in real output per person.

THE FATAL FLAW

The failure to recognize the primary role of wage increases in excess of productivity as the principal initiator of inflation since the system settled down after the Korean War was the fatal flaw in economic theory and, by extension, public policy. Monetarists like Milton Friedman recognized that the market for labor had been altered by legislation and regulation. In his book *Free to Choose*, where he discusses how the labor market operates, he says: "Here, too, interference by government, through min-imum wages, for example, or trade unions through restricting entry, may distort the information transmitted or may prevent individuals from free-ly acting on that information."[5]

Quite so! But having observed and objected to the rigidities in the la-bor market due to government intervention, he proceeded to ignore the connection between wages and prices by denying the existence of cost-push inflation. He pretended that the system was self-regulating and that equilibrium would be restored by some invisible hand. Yet even after two disastrous recessions and one inadequate recovery since *Free to Choose* was written, the kind of free market he dreamed of and wrote about did not exist.

The Friedman analysis of where capitalism went wrong and his con-clusion that business cycles were caused by monetary excesses is ex-actly what I believe. His concern that governmental intervention had reached the point where it actually impeded the satisfaction of human needs struck a sympathetic chord and was consistent with my experi-ence in the business world. But his solution to the problem of inflation was one that ignored the rigidities that he deplored. For him labor was just another price determined in the free market.

This blind spot has been noted by many critics. In *Capitalism's In-flation and Unemployment Crisis*, Sidney Weintraub says: "To interpret money wages as 'simply another price' is to mistake flies for elephants." A general wage rise "comprises about 55 percent of gross business costs, closer to 75 percent net costs, and probably even more of vari-able costs."[6]

In view of this, one should not underestimate the significance of Dr. Friedman's unsubstantiated contention that "wage increases in excess of increases in productivity are a result of inflation, rather than the cause."[7] The Main Economic Indicators show that wages outstripped productivity in the United States every year from 1964 to 1991. Therein lies the princi-pal source of inflation for that period.

Not only have wages moved up faster than productivity from at least as far back as 1958, they outpaced prices in 18 or the 21 years – the excep-tions being '70, '74, and '79 – prior to the time Milton and Rose Friedman first published *Free to Choose* in 1980. The wage index for that entire peri-od – of which the 1964-1991 segment can be seen in Figure 2 – has kept well ahead of the price index.

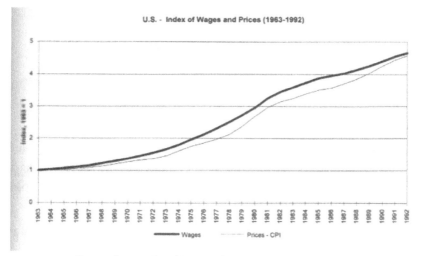

Source: International Financial Statistics Yearbook 1993, IMF

Milton Friedman's totally irrational endorsement of zero cash reserves, and his naïve acceptance of his conclusion that all inflation is monetary inflation was the key that unlocked a Pandora's Box of banking and financial innovation. The bankers loved him and lauded him because they gained an unprecedented freedom from rules and restrictions.

Looking at the banks new licences for unbridled greed from the eyes of the 99 percent of the world's people was entirely different. Banks had long been among the most profitable businesses in the world and suddenly they were given the freedom to extract an even bigger pound of flesh. It is my opinion that the ideas of Milton Friedman have been responsible for more pain and grief than those of any other economist in living history. He is primarily responsible for a financial mess for which there is no precedent.

AN INNOVATIVE ERA OF MONETARY MADNESS

When banks were no longer required to have cash reserves it became obvious that there should be some restraint or anyone would be able to incorporate a bank. So someone invented the idea of "capital adequacy." But what is that? How much capital is enough? Anything less than 20 or 30 percent would only be a token in the case of a major meltdown so the banks turned to the Bank for International Settlements and its Basel I, II, and finally III for a level of about 5 percent to placate the monetary wolf pack. Five percent is just a token. The powerful bankers lobby was successful in keeping the realists at bay.

Even this inadequate minimum was not properly enforced. Bank leverage in the U.S. soared from about 12 ½ to 1 in 1974 to 25 or 30 to 1 in the 1980s.

GREED KNOWS NO BOUNDS

One would think that their licenses "to create" $20,000 in accounts receivable for every $1,000 capital invested would be so embarrassingly lucrative that the banksters would just keep silent and enjoy their vast fortunes. But that is not so. More than enough is never enough! They are constantly looking for new corners to cut in their persistent efforts to rob the public.

Looking back at some old files I re-read about bank collusion in commercial fraud cases like Enron and then later WorldCom. These major scandals stoked cocktail conversation for months. But in a way these outstanding cases were only the tip of a much more ominous iceberg - widespread cheating by many of the most prestigious firms on Wall Street.

The list read like a Who's Who of world finance; Merrill, Credit Suisse Group's CSFB, Morgan Stanley, Goldman Sachs, Bear Stearns, J.P. Morgan Chase, Lehman Brothers and U.S. Bancorp. At firm after firm, according to prosecutors, analysts wittingly duped investors to curry favor with corporate clients. Investment houses received secret payments from companies they gave strong recommendations to buy. And for top executives whose companies were clients, stock underwriters offered special access to hot initial public offerings, according to the *New York Times*.[8]

Brian Miller, writing in the Toronto *Globe and Mail*, said: "There's little repentance on Wall Street these days. Even after 10 major securities firms agreed to pay a combined $1.4 billion in penalties and costs to put the scandal behind them - a tiny fraction of their profits during that era - not one had admitted any wrongdoing and probably never will."[9]

Fast forward to more recent times I found a clipping entitled **"Settlement talks heat up at JP Morgan. Bank head Jamie Dimon meets with U.S. Attorney-General Eric Holder in attempt to broker $11-billion deal to end federal scrutiny,"** an article by David Henry and David Ingram that appeared in the Toronto *Globe and Mail* on September 27, 2013.

"J.P. Morgan Chase & Co. chief executive Jamie Dimon met Thursday morning with U.S. Attorney-General Eric Holder as the nation's biggest bank attempts to end investigations into its sales of shoddy mortgage securities leading up to the financial crisis.

"The bank and federal and state authorities are trying to resolve the probes with a potential $11-billion (U.S.) settlement, according to sources familiar with the matter.

"After the meeting with the U.S. Justice Department, which lasted about an hour, Mr. Holder told reporters that he had met with representatives of J.P. Morgan but did not mention Mr. Dimon by name. He declined to give details of the talks.

"Speaking at a press conference on an unrelated topic, the Attorney-General also said that the Justice Department plans to make announcements in the coming weeks and months."[10]

A couple of months later a deal was reached with JP Morgan that involved a $13 billion settlement. A headline in a report by TheRealNews.com "**Documents in JP Morgan settlement reveal how every large bank in U.S. has committed mortgage fraud.**" A conversation between Jaisal Noor, TRNN Producer and Bill Black, an associate professor of economics and law at the University of Missouri-Kansas City, and author of *The Best Way to Rob a Bank Is to Own One*, begins as follows:

"Black: So, this'll be the first installment in what we can learn from the statement of facts that constitutes J.P. Morgan's admissions. This is the settlement that the Department of Justice is billing as the $13 billion settlement. As I've explained in the past, it's not that big, but it's still quite large in dollar terms. And we owe a debt of gratitude to Judge Jed Rakoff, who's been giving the Securities and Exchange Commission a hard time about settling cases and getting absolutely no useful admissions from the people that perpetrated the frauds.

"And so the Justice Department was embarrassed into getting this statement of fact, which was obviously closely negotiated with J.P. Morgan to try to not establish its criminal liability, but still is a remarkable document in terms of what it tells us about the fraud second epidemics, not just at J.P. Morgan, but also criminality at Washington Mutual and at Bear Stearns. And it tells us about the whole secondary market frauds. And it tells us a great deal about why the Justice Department is batting .000 against the elite frauds."[11]

Tax evasion is another piece of the financial puzzle. "**Swiss bankers helped hide billions from U.S. taxes, senators say.**"

The first three paragraphs of this article by Tanya Talaga, Global economics reporter, that appeared in the *Toronto Star* on February 27, 2014, read as follows:

"Like a scene out of a spy novel, U.S. senators claim Swiss bankers slipped into America on tourist visas, held meetings with potential clients in secret elevators and even passed a bank statement inside a sports magazine to a customer at a swank Manhattan restaurant.

"The clandestine moves were done in an attempt to help U.S.-Swiss bank account holders keep from paying taxes to Uncle Sam, a Senate subcommittee probe charges.

"As of 2006, 22,000 Americans had assets worth nearly $12 billion hidden away at Credit Suisse, the vast majority of that money undeclared, according to the senator's report, released late Tuesday."[12]

This practice of moving money offshore to avoid paying domestic taxes is extremely widespread. A book entitled *Treasure Islands: Uncovering the Damage of Offshore Banking and Tax Havens*[13] by Nicholas Shaxson, paints an incredible picture.

He describes the techniques by which one jurisdiction after another is persuaded to provide either a special deal or total exemption for foreign money invested in their jurisdiction. The total amounts involved number in the trillions of dollars.

Shaxson asks rhetorically, "What is the largest offshore island haven?" The answer: "Manhattan."

The list of unfair tricks appears to be never-ending. In an article entitled "The Leveraged Buyout of America," Ellen Brown JD, describes a development that I consider to be totally scandalous. It reads in part as follows:

"In a letter to Federal Reserve Chairman Ben Bernanke dated June 27, 2013, US Representative Alan Grayson and three co-signers expressed concern about the expansion of large banks into what have traditionally been non-financial commercial spheres.

"Specifically: [W]e are concerned about how large banks have recently expanded their businesses into such fields as electric power production, oil refining and distribution, owning and operating of public assets such as ports and airports, and even uranium mining.

"After listing some disturbing examples, they observed:

"According to legal scholar Saule Omarova, over the past five years, there has been a 'quiet transformation of U.S. financial holding companies.' These financial services companies have become global merchants that seek to extract rent from any commercial or financial business activity within their reach. They have used legal authority in Graham-Leach-Bliley to subvert the 'foundational principle of separation of banking from commerce.'

"It seems like there is a significant macro-economic risk in having a massive entity like, say J.P. Morgan, both issuing credit cards and mortgages, managing municipal bond offerings, selling gasoline and electric power, running large oil tankers, trading derivatives, and owning and operating airports, in multiple countries.

"A 'macro' risk indeed – not just to our economy but to our democracy and our individual and national sovereignty. Giant banks are buying up our country's infrastructure – the power and supply chains that are vital to the economy. Aren't there rules against that? And where are the banks getting the money?"[16]

Another article by Ellen Brown entitled "**The Global Banking Game Is Rigged, and the FDIC Is Suing,**" exposes two other scandalous practices – interest rate swaps and rigged interest rates:

"Taxpayers are paying billions of dollars for a swindle pulled off by the world's biggest banks, using a form of derivative called interest-rate swaps; and the Federal Deposit Insurance Corporation has now joined a chorus of litigants suing over it. According to an SEIU report (http://www.seiu.org/images/pdfs/Interest%20Rate20Swap%20Report%2003%2022%202010.pdf):

"Derivatives … have turned into a windfall for banks and a nightmare for taxpayers … While banks are still collecting fixed rates of 3 to 6 percent, they are now regularly paying public entities as little as a tenth of one percent on the outstanding bonds, with rates expected to remain low in the future. Over the life of the deals, banks are now projected to collect billions more than they pay state and local governments – an outcome which amounts to a second bailout for banks, this one paid directly out of state and local budgets.

"It is not just that local governments, universities and pension funds made a bad bet on these swaps. The game itself was rigged. The FDIC is now suing in civil court for damages and punitive damages, a lead that other injured local governments and agencies would be well-advised to follow. But they need to hurry, because time on the statute of limitations is running out.

The Largest Cartel in World History: On March 14, 2014, the FDIC filed suit for LIBOR-rigging against sixteen of the world's largest banks – including the three largest US banks (JP Morgan Chase, Bank of America, and Citigroup), the three largest UK banks, the largest German bank, the largest Japanese bank, and several of the largest Swiss banks. Bill Black, professor of law and economics and a former bank fraud investigator, calls (http://www.youtube.com/watch?v=Rn5JclFHglc#t=196) them "the largest cartel in world history, by at least three and probably four orders of magnitude."

"LIBOR (the London Interbank Offering Rate) is the benchmark rate by which banks themselves can borrow. It is a crucial rate involved in hundreds of trillions of dollars in derivative trades, and it is set by these sixteen megabanks privately and in secret.

"Interest rate swaps are now a $426 trillion (http://www.business-week.com/articles/2014-02-27/interest-rate-swaps-trading-comes-out-of-the-shadows) business. That's trillion with a "t" – about seven times the gross domestic product of all the countries in the world combined. According to the Office of the Comptroller of the Currency, in 2012 US banks held $183.7 trillion in interest-rate contracts, with only four firms representing 93% of total derivative holdings; and three of the four were JP Morgan Chase, Citigroup, and Bank of America, the US banks being sued by the FDIC over manipulation of LIBOR."[15]

The case against the banking cartel and international financial system could go on and on. But what I have said is more than enough to prove that the curse of monetarism, or Friedmanism as it is sometimes called, should be erased from the face of the planet.

Professor Friedman didn't even accomplish his stated mission of getting governments out of the banking and financial systems. When the system was deliberately crashed again in 2008 taxpayers had to ride to the rescue of big banks and big business to the tune of hundreds of billions of dollars. Actually the figures were many times larger than the public was aware of as we shall see when we get to the Federal Reserve System.

Money is the gasoline that fires the economic engine. To give private corporations a monopoly to create money is total insanity. To let them create all that money as debt that has to be repaid with interest goes beyond total insanity if that is possible. It is a crime against humanity!

The giants have to be brought down to normal size and the Cartel dissolved. The big Wall Street, City of London and other giant banks can only get away with their blatant grand larceny as part of a larger group that dances to the same piper. The cartel comprises the giant banks, the Bank for International Settlements (BIS), the Bank for Reconstruction and Development (World Bank), the International Monetary Fund (IMF), and a worldwide network of central banks of which the U.S. Federal Reserve System (Fed) is the most notorious, powerful, and inimical to the public welfare – both in the U.S. and internationally. Of this list, the BIS, IMF and Fed should all be "terminated" on the basis that their net benefit to the human species is negative. It should begin with the BIS which is the nerve center of the whole system – the switchboard through which the

people who run the system disseminate their decisions.

CHAPTER EIGHT

THE CORONAVIRUS CATASTROPHE

"Go home, stay home, save lives."
— The Government of Canada

The Coronavirus catastrophe just seemed to sneak into our consciousness like a thief in the night. It wasn't long, however, until it became the longest running top news story since World War II. Perhaps that is because it was war of a kind. It was obviously a virus that could be used in warfare and the fact that all of the major powers, and some of the minor ones, are deeply involved in these endeavors is proof positive of the moral bankruptcy of our political leadership.

Very soon I realized that something unique in my lifetime was happening and that perhaps I should record a little of the story. I knew that there would be financial consequences of catastrophic proportions and that was one more reason for keeping tabs on what was happening.

It was only on May 26, 2020, that I saw in print what I had long suspected. The headline in GMWATCH read as follows:

> "Chinese and US scientists genetically engineered bat coronaviruses in dangerous gain-of-function research stretching back years"

Research was omitted from landmark paper claiming natural origin of SaRS-CoV-2. Report: Claire Robinson

> "Chinese and US scientists have been collaborating for years in dangerous gain-of-function experiments that involve genetically engineering coronaviruses from bats and other animals, as revealed by a series of scientific publications. The coronaviruses are related to the SARS viruses that cause severe acute respiratory diseases in humans. The scientists were based at the Wuhan Institute of Virology (WIV) in China, the lab suspected by some of accidentally releasing the SaRS-CoV-2 virus that caused the COVID-19 pandemic, and at the University of North Carolina (UNC) in the US."

This news is proof positive that there is no solution to our problems except worldwide disarmament!

Question for the day. Why should taxpayers have to pay for the design and development of new viruses that might eventually kill them?

The first Canadian case of COVID-19 was confirmed on January 27th, 2020 after a man who had returned to Toronto from Wuhan, Hubei, China tested positive. But it was just another story as far as my wife Sandra and I were concerned. We never even thought of cancelling a much needed winter vacation in St. Lucia at the end of February, returning on March 6th. We had stayed at the Body Holiday Hotel in St. Lucia that we had found by accident a year earlier and found it to be a wonderful spot to bind the mind and body together in wholesome harmony.

The repeat performance had achieved its goal and we were in high good humors when we got home to Toronto. It pleased us that we would be able to attend the condo bridge club on Tuesday evening and play our first game of the season with our friends Mary and "Doc" who had returned to the city from their off-the-grid summer establishment to a rental condo next door to ours. We had a great evening except that we were used to winning but that night they clobbered us. Just as we were leaving early to watch the nine o'clock news Mary whispered that it was her birthday so I led the whole room in "Happy Birthday to You".

The following day, March 11th, Prime Minister Justin Trudeau announced a $1 billion response fund including $500 million to go to the provinces and territories, a $50 million contribution to the World Health Organization, and an additional $275 million to fund COVID research in Canada. That same evening the WHO declared the existence of a global pandemic.

Whammy! The World we knew had come to a sudden end. No more bridge or book club, no more baseball, basketball and football. No more Church on Sunday, big weddings or traditional funerals, no more ballet or opera, no more breakfast meetings of a handful of us seniors who find comfort and inspiration from just being together. Our World had changed inexorably and the worst was yet to come.

THE PANDEMIC

The newspapers kept publishing so we were able to get our morning briefing. The Condo Board wouldn't let "Old Faithful" deliver the paper to the door at the crack of dawn as had been done for decades. Instead we had to go down to the concierge to pick it up from the tabletop where they were all neatly laid out. This turned out to be a blessing because it provided a reason to get up and going before breakfast. The evening television news provided our daily nightmare of statistics and all the bad that had happened across the country with a few inserts from the U.S. and elsewhere.

Our first nightmare was that we were not prepared. We only had a few masks and a handful of inhalators. I will never forget the look of frustration and fear on the part of the nurses and the other care workers. They simply didn't have the equipment to do their jobs properly and many of them didn't mind saying so on camera. I could imagine how they would feel going home to a family of young or old people, or both, not knowing whether or not you might have been infected by the virus as a consequence of your dedications to help others. Shivers go up and down my spine every time I think about it.

The first responders found themselves in a similar dilemma. They didn't have the proper clothing, shields, high quality masks essential to respond to a call that was quite likely to be inflicted with the virus. It just isn't fair. But what are the alternatives? There are none! So off they go, sirens screaming, knowing all too well that they may be putting their own lives, as well as that of their family, in jeopardy.

The nightly telecasts had their own morbid rhythm. We were bombarded with statistics, separate from the front line, specialist doctors answering question after question about the virus, how we could best avoid getting infected, should we wear masks? The answer ranged from no, to maybe, then possibly yes. Their principal advice was in respect of working. If your work isn't essential, go home and stay home.

CANADIANS COME HOME

Meanwhile the federal government had suggested that Canadians outside Canada should come home at once. The mass movement began at once. Both of my sons were in the U.S. at the time and had to alter their time of return. Peter, the elder son and his wife Catherine, had been in the Florida Keys because he finds it a wonderful place to indulge in his passion of Scuba diving. They drove home in two days – a record – and said the first day was miserable due to the millions of snowbirds heading north. (A "snowbird" for the benefit of my American friends, is the word we use to describe the hordes of Canadians, mostly from our French speaking province of Quebec, but a few from elsewhere, who always spend their winters in Florida).

My younger son David and his wife Katherine own a condo on the Gulf side of Florida, they decided to stay put for a few days to enjoy the warm weather. And then they headed for home. Their only penalty was spending the first night in a one star hotel, and not being able to get any food other than hot dogs and hamburgers, otherwise it was smooth sailing.

In both cases they observed the mandatory 14-day quarantine. In both cases their homes had been well stocked by their families who made sure they were well looked after until they were free to begin shopping for themselves.

Canadians who were in the U.S. had little problem getting home. The same good luck did not apply to those from overseas. There were quite a few Canadian Nationals in Wuhan who were desperate to return home. On February 2, the Canadian Armed Forces announced that it planned to charter a plane to assist in the evacuation. Only those who had entered China on a Canadian passport would be allowed to take the flight. When authorization from the Chinese government had been obtained, the coveted flight of Canadian nationals and permanent residents took off. The plane landed at Canadian Forces Base Trenton on February 7 for screening and quarantine of the passengers.

On February 21 another chartered flight rescued 131 Canadians who were quarantined aboard The Diamond Princess, a cruise ship docked in Japan. I saw several pictures of passengers signalling from their cabins, pleading for help, and appearing more and more desperate as the days passed. It must have been similar to being in jail. One can imagine their relief when all those who tested negative for the virus were released and flown to CFB Trenton for processing.

There were other flights but the majority had to fend for themselves. Scheduled flights were being cancelled daily, leaving passengers scrambling to find a seat or two on another airline. According to numerous reports the frustration was almost unbearable. Insult was added to injury when a seat did become available only to find that the fare had increased dramatically compared to the one originally booked. Boo to the gangster who took advantage of desperate people in their time of crisis.

No doubt there are people who will disagree with me but I thought the federal government did a better than average job in handling the transportation file.

THE PRIVILEGED FEW

There is no doubt that my wife Sandra and I are among the privileged few. We have a two-storey condominium overlooking the Toronto

Harbour with its rim of islands across the bay. The view is magnificent and our windows are just like a giant television because there is always something going on day and night all year round. I bought it 40 years ago for cost when there was a dip in the housing market and the builder was short of cash. It normally gets a lot of use for visitors from everywhere to the point where we have dubbed it the Hellyer Hilton. Now it is quiet.

Sandra and I are both seniors so we were aware from the outset that we were in the ranks of those most vulnerable. Sandra's son-in-law, a professor of biology at Western University in London, Ontario, wrote a brief paper on the COVID-19 and ended by saying that we were both in the most vulnerable group and if we were to be infected by the virus we would either be very ill or die. It's always nice to have a professional opinion.

We have been very careful from the outset and established a routine. Sandra is a very early riser who begins her journaling at the crack of dawn. I follow about a half an hour later, get the paper, have a huge cereal and fruit breakfast, share a few minutes of the daily Biblical reflections with Sandra, and then get to work at about 9:00 AM. I had started this book in February, but ran into some glitches and didn't really accomplish very much until the lockdown was in effect.

Every day Sandra and I walked around our three-building complex. At breakfast we look at the weather and pick the best time for this daily exercise. The weather has been cold and windy but we haven't missed a day yet. If the wind is coming from the East we go around the building clockwise. If we have a West wind we go counter-clockwise.

We celebrated Earth day, April 22, by taking a bag with us to pick up the refuse as we walked along. The treasures included a man's hat, the worse for wear, a single rubber glove, several pop cans and other goodies. We were wearing gloves of course. The bag was about three quarters full by the time we finished our circuit.

Another blessing we enjoyed were wide sidewalks or equivalent all the way around our complex, so it was easy to keep the required social distance and almost all of our neighbours did the same. Once in a while a bicycle would whip by within arms length, and a couple of times someone would be texting and not watch where they were going. The penalty for jay-walking should apply!

SATURDAYS, SUNDAYS & HOLIDAYS

For most of last year I was not allowed to work on Saturday morning, but when I started to write my fourth "last book" in February Sandra agreed to make an exception until it was complete. But Saturday afternoon was our time together for fun of one kind or another. Usually it was a matinee with sometimes dinner out after the movie. When the lockdown ended that option we were lucky to have an alternative.

My late wife Ellen and I were the last people on our street to get television. We were the last to get colored television. You would be correct, then, in assuming that my second wife Sandra, widow of my best friend ever, and I would be the last to get Netflix – despite the rave reviews. It was our very good fortune, however, that my elder son Peter and his wife Catherine had generously given us a one year subscription last Christmas, and their son Josh was delighted to install it for us. So Sandra and I agreed that it would be "Saturday afternoon at Netflix." It was a Godsend!

Our benefactors had also given us a list of their favourite shows with *The Crown* at the top of the list. So we decided to try it first. There was a bit of bias on my part because my late wife Ellen and I had been fortunate enough to have seats in Westminster Abbey on the occasion of the Coronation of the present Queen Elizabeth on June 2, 1953. It was also our pleasure to be responsible for her safety and welfare on a couple of occasions when a visit to Canada included time to review one of the units of the Canadian Armed Forces.

So we began to watch the episodes of *The Crown* beginning with the first episode of the first season and working our way along. Sandra and I both enjoyed them immensely, some more than others, especially subjects like the Suez Crisis or the Profumo Affair and other events that occurred when I was in active politics. Once in a while we slipped in an extra episode and once or twice on a Sunday afternoon as well.

Sunday is a very special day for us. We are churchgoers and miss being able to meet in worship with our many friends and acquaintances. We were especially nostalgic as we approached Palm Sunday and Easter. Then to our delight we learned that an effort would be made to live stream the virtual services. One of our choristers, Pat Thompson, in collaboration with one of our two ministers, laid out the plans for an extremely complicated series of connections from sources miles apart.

Their remarkable talent, along with those of the numerous participants, came to fruition on Sunday March 22nd. There were a couple of tiny glitches, but by Palm Sunday everything was perfect. Our wireless wizards even had parishioners appearing to parade with their palm branches in hand. Sandra and I found the link and enjoyed the excitement. Minutes later one of us pushed a wrong button and lost control. We paid a heavy price.

The Easter Sunday broadcast was absolutely perfect and after that it became routine. I usually go back to bed for an hour after breakfast to make up a bit of the shortfall in sleep due to too much problem-solving at night. Just after 10:00 AM I get dressed, put on the clothes that I normally wear on Sunday, go down for the paper and then join Sandra as we sit side by side in front of her laptop. At 11:00 AM the organ (or piano) prelude begins followed by a call to worship by Rev. Jason Meyers. A member of the congregation reads the scripture from wherever he or she may be; a special musical number followed by a sermon by our wonderful preacher Rev. Karen Bowles, etc.

Usually there is a bit of humor when Jason Meyers asks the children to come forward; with a bit of encouragement the Meyers' two adorable boys Isaiah and Simon seem to fly on stage, one from each side. They participate in the dialogue but every once in a while you see a tongue stuck out, or a wave to the audience and you get your free smile for the day.

The wondrous reality is that Toronto's Metropolitan United Church is not the only congregation that is being forced together in this way. There are literally dozens of churches, mosques, synagogues and temples that are keeping the faith virtually. Veteran soldiers can tell you "there are no atheists in the trenches." So in this deadly war of a very different kind there is no harm in putting in a word to the Creator.

INNOVATION & RECREATION

There is nothing like a coronavirus pandemic to get people thinking and acting outside of the box. One of the earliest and best examples was one that my wife noticed in the Business section of the *Toronto Star*, April 1, 2020, that had been written by Phoebe Wall Howard in the *Detroit Free Press*. The article titled "**Hairstylist and doctors played key role in design of Ford face shield.**" It reads in part:

> "It sounds like a Hollywood movie script. It was, in fact, real life in Detroit in the time of the novel coronavirus.
>
> Ford Motor Co. executives issued a call to action March 19, after receiving an alert from the Mayo Clinic. Ford immediately assembled a task force to address the personal protective equipment shortage.
>
> Within hours, the automaker decided to pivot from building cars to manufacturing medical devices, setting into motion the first steps that would generate tens of thousands of protective face shields for doctors, nurses and first responders during the rapid-

ly spreading pandemic that causes respiratory crisis. Within one week, a small team of designers from a shop within the company called D-Ford would collaborate virtually to review plans, design prototypes, build the early designs, meet with doctors, test prototypes, redesign, re-test and redesign."[1]

The result was tens of thousands of face shields that would help save the lives of first responders and health care workers in the line of duty.

I was particularly interested in this phenomenon as it was precisely the one adopted during World War II when automobile, refrigerator and washing machine plants were converted into armaments plants to help win the war. I have long been promoting the reverse, that is converting all the armament plants into zero point energy heater and engines to heat our houses, power our cars, trucks, tractors, boats and airplanes in order to win the war of saving our planet from further overheating!

In my province of Ontario there have been many businesses that have converted to the manufacture of shields, masks, and protective clothing for use by the nurses, doctors, paramedics and other first line troopers in the war against the deadly COVID-19.

A real joy of the otherwise trying situation is to see the myriad examples of compassion and goodness in the human species. A Toronto butcher posted a sign offering free meat to the poor. The internet is packed with entertainment of all sorts. I have heard some of the finest choral music one could want to hear. Some of it has been done digitally with 20 or 30 singers all participating from their own homes, a masterpiece of harmonic co-ordination.

Forgive me for being parochial, but Sandra's granddaughter Hannah Kim, in her role as Luna Li, recorded a number of alternatives from harp to guitar in her unique and beguiling manner so popular with her many fans. And finally those Irish ladies singing and dancing in the street to provide cheer to the elderly ladies who had so little to cheer about. So far, mostly music. But three cheers and a tiger to all the wonderfully creative puzzles and games for the children who were so desperate for a little fun to relieve the boredom.

FROM PURE LOVE AND COMPASSION TO INDESCRIBABLE EVIL

It was almost news time and someone said there has been a terrible shooting. "In the U.S.?" I asked in my knee-jerk reaction. "No, in Canada," was the response. The news came on and for the first time in weeks the lead story was not the coronavirus, and the numbers of new cases. It was a mass shooting in Nova Scotia, one of our Atlantic provinces.

Incredible! It wasn't that we had never had a mass shooting in Canada, but they were extremely rare. A native-born Nova Scotian driving a Royal Canadian Mounted Police cruiser, and wearing an RCMP uniform had gunned down 13 people. Gabriel Wortman's killing spree began with an argument and an assault on his girlfriend. It ended 13 hours later and 100 kilometres away with a chilling 22 dead in rural Nova Scotia.

The girlfriend's family came in from the woods where she had been hiding and eventually a 911 call came in about a shooting near Portapique, where the saga began. Police driving to the chaotic scene found a man who said he had been shot while driving by someone in a passing vehicle "that looked like a police vehicle."

"Just imagine," said Tom Taggart, a councillor with the municipality of Colchester which encompasses Portapique. "Imagine the panic, the fear and the anxiety of the residents and of the police trying to protect." Taggart said he spoke to one resident who described the scene "like a war zone". That is exactly what it looked like, burned out houses and barns, burned cars and trucks, and bodies along the road. To the best of my knowledge there has never been anything comparable in Canadian history.

The casualty first reported RCMP Constable Heidi Stephenson, a career officer with a strong work ethic, who left behind her husband Dean and children Connor and Ava. A report filed a week later told of her incredible bravery. "She was a hero," said Brian Sauvé, head of the union representing 20,000 RCMP members across Canada.[2] The whole saga had been one of considerable mayhem.

The shock was palpable. It extended right across the country. Flags flew at half-mast. A beautiful young piper played "Amazing Grace." Several singers composed songs of consolation. I have never seen so many flowers and stuffed animals piled at the crash sites in an outpouring of love and respect. But how could this have happened? Most Canadians are nice but Nova Scotians have their own unique brand of niceness as anyone who has ever visited the province would know.

There were some questions asked as to why the police had not used a province-wide alert? And if they had, would some lives been saved? But it was a crime scene unlike any other and Nova Scotians seemed more concerned with consoling the families whose lives had been forever torn in one incredible awful night. Everyone would pull together in an outpouring of love.

The funeral services had to be tailor made to meet the needs of the Coronavirus Pandemic. A private service was planned for Constable Stephenson. Normally she would have received a regimental funeral but COVID-19 made that impossible.

DOUBLE WHAMMY

Canadians were still struggling with the horrific mass shooting when a Canadian Forces CH-148 helicopter crashed in full view of multiple witnesses on HMCS Fredericton. The helicopter was just returning from a training flight and was only moments away from a scheduled landing aboard HMCS Fredericton when it went down in full view of horrified shipmates who were preparing to receive it aboard the frigate in the Ionian Sea off Greece.

All six people aboard – four aircrew and two sailors – were killed when the chopper went down in water roughly 3,000 metres deep. Only one body was recovered, that of Sub-Lt. Abbigail Cowborough the 23 year old sailor from Halifax. The warship recovered the helicopter's flight safety recorders which were designed to break away and float to the surface after a crash. These devices were sent to the National Research Council for analysis in Ottawa.[4]

A week later Canadians from coast to coast to coast watched as six members of the Armed Forces who had been killed in the crash were welcomed home in a special ramp ceremony at Canadian Forces Base Trenton in Ontario. Reminders of COVID-19 were everywhere as the ceremony began, from the sparse crowd outside CFB Trenton to the masks and physical distancing of the victims families. Military personnel and government leaders on hand included Governor General Julie Payette and Prime Minister Justin Trudeau.

The pandemic wasn't the only difference from previous ramp ceremonies, which started in their modern form during the decades-long war in Afghanistan. There were also the pillows and military headdresses, a reminder that the remains of most of those lost here have not been recovered.

Soon the huge C-17 Globemaster landed and taxied to the loading area. The first to emerge was the casket of Sub-Lt. Abbigail Cowborough carried by eight military pallbearers to the sound of a lone bagpipe playing a lament. Next was the pillow and headdress of Capt. Brenden Ian MacDonald, followed by those of Capt. Kevin Hagen, Capt. Maxime Miron-Morin, Sub-Lt. Matthew Pyke, and finally Master Cpl. Matthew

Cousins. Each was placed in a waiting hearse to drive out of CFB Trenton, past a column of saluting troops as they began the traditional voyage down the Highway of Heroes.

THE PANDEMIC PARADOX

As of the time of writing 3.79 million people worldwide have been infected and there are new cases daily. The death toll, to date, is 263,600. Our American cousins are having a rough time. The country is divided on the extent of restrictive measures that should remain in force. These numbers will be dramatically changed by the time this book is published.

In Canada, the government that has been telling us to go home, stay home and save lives has now reversed the message and tells us to go out, enjoy the fresh air, and stay safe. The formula for achieving that has not yet been made public.

One thing we do know is that the old folk living in seniors' residences are dying by the dozens. The group homes are understaffed and one of the most poignant stories I have heard was that of the one last nurse leaving a home. She was ill with the virus. But before she left she donned full protective gear and went to dress the sores of a patient in pain. Bravo.

Governments at all levels have realized that they have failed the seniors by understaffing, ridiculously low wages and lack of inspection. Whenever budgets were inadequate, the seniors' homes became an easy target. If talk means anything this desperate situation will be set right in the future. Meanwhile staff are being transferred from some hospitals and the Armed Forces have been brought in to assist in a number of cases.

At this point readers may wonder what the Coronavirus Pandemic has got to do with money and banking. The answer, in a word, is EVERYTHING!

ONE MORE FINANCIAL TRAGEDY

The Toronto Stock Exchange S&P/TSX in a bull market reached a peak of 17,970 on Feb. 20/20. The following day it reversed for a few days, then a minor rally, and finally reached a low of 11,228 on March 23, down 37.8% from the high.[5] In just over a month people who had saved most of their lives to provide a decent income in their senior years had lost more than a third of their savings. Our American friends were in the same boat.

I didn't comment on this earlier because very few people were talking about it. What they did know was the economy had collapsed, and all the economists were saying that when the crisis was over we would be in a prolonged and deep recession, perhaps the worst since the Great Depression. Jobs have been wiped out, the majority of small businesses are in jeopardy. Escaping the downturn will be a steep and difficult climb.

It would be easy for me to say "What did you expect?" We have a bubble economy. It has no substance. The Pandemic was the needle that punctured the balloon and the poor people of the world will have to work very hard to fill it with fresh air and start the process of reflation. This is because, as Einstein said; "It is a form of insanity to keep doing the same thing over and over again and expect different results." The question I am posing is: "When will sanity prevail?"

GOVERNMENTS COME TO THE RESCUE WITH BAND-AID MEASURES

On March 27, 2020 President Donald Trump signed the "Coronavirus Aid, Relief and Economic Recovery Act" (CARES Act) into law.

As Ellen Brown points out the *Act* will result in doling out $2.2 trillion in crisis relief, most of it going to Corporate America with few strings attached. Beyond that the Federal Reserve is making over $4 trillion available to banks, hedge funds and other financial entities of all stripes; it has dropped the Fed funds rate (the rate at which banks borrow from each other) effectively to zero; and it has made $1.5 trillion available to the rest of the market. So the people at the top of the income scale will be well taken care of. The working people of America, Canada, and most of the rest of the world will not.

The principal purpose of this book is to provide a plan that will change the balance of power and provide a better deal for the 99% of the population who have been seriously neglected for so long.

CHAPTER NINE

THE BIGGEST HEIST IN HISTORY

"The Federal Reserve (privately-owned banks) are one of the most corrupt institutions the world has ever seen."
– Senator Louis T. McFadden (For 22 years
Chairman of the U.S. Banking and Currency Commission)

The Fed, as you may not know, but might guess from the haste with which it rides to the rescue of the big New York banks when they are in trouble, was the brainchild of the barons of Wall Street. Taking a leaf from the memoirs of John D. Rockefeller Sr., who loudly proclaimed that he didn't like competition, and proved the validity of his thesis by buying up or making deals with his competitors, the heads of New York's most powerful banks concluded that genuine competition was not a profitable policy. So they decided to do something about it.

A small, select group organized a very secret meeting at the private resort of J.P. Morgan on Jekyll Island, off the coast of Georgia. There, in the atmosphere of a mystery thriller, they agreed on an audacious plan. Their scheme, devised by Paul M. Warburg, and subsequently adopted by Congress, was the creation of a legal private monopoly to control the U.S. money supply for the benefit of the few under the guise of protecting and promoting the public interest.

"The seven men who attended the secret meeting on Jekyll Island, where the Federal Reserve System was conceived, represented an estimated one-fourth of the total wealth of the entire world. The group comprised of: Nelson W. Aldrich, Henry P. Davison, Charles D. Norton, Abraham P. Andrew, Frank A. Vanderlip, Benjamin Strong and Paul M. Warburg," as recorded on page 24 of *The Creature from Jekyll Island: A Second Look at the Federal Reserve* by G. Edward Griffin.[1] Even a quick scan of the names and their connections is enough to convince one that their "creation" was not designed to be in the interests of the American people.

It is a tribute to the skill of the international bankers that they were able to draft a bill, revise it, change its name and make the few window-dressing compromises necessary to get it adopted by Congress just before

Christmas in 1913 when quite a few Representatives must have been dreaming of sugar plum fairies instead of exercising due diligence. Only Congressman Charles Lindberg Sr. seemed to grasp the essence of what was going on.

To put it bluntly, the Congress transferred its sovereign constitutional right to create money to the sole custody of a small group of private bankers. The magnitude of the heist is unprecedented in the history of the world – the numbers now are in the high trillions.

THERE WAS AN ALTERNATIVE

If, instead of copying some European experiments, the U.S. had established a publicly-owned central bank mandated to serve the interests of the American people, the U.S. federal debt could have been zero today, instead of $26 trillion and rising. There would have been no interminable wrangling about increasing debt limits, and budgets could have been addressed rationally. But that is what might have been. This book is dedicated to what has to be done to reverse the damage before it becomes fatal.

Soon after the Federal Reserve bill was passed, the magnitude of the tragedy began to be recognized. William Jennings Bryan, who acted as Democrat whip, later said: "In my long political career, the one thing I genuinely regret is my part in getting the banking and currency legislation (Federal Reserve Act of 1913) enacted into law."[2] President Woodrow Wilson, just 3 years after passage of the Act, wrote: "A great industrial nation is controlled by its system of credit. Our system of credit is concentrated (in the Federal Reserve System). The growth of the nation, therefore, and all our activities are in the hands of a few men.... We have come to be one of the worst ruled, one of the most completely controlled and dominated governments in the civilized world."[3] But the bill was not repealed; now, more than 100 years later, the sell-out is still the law. This makes you wonder what the people's representatives have been doing to earn their salaries.

The people in charge of the original deception were very far-seeing. They realized that when future governments had to borrow from them they would need a constant income stream to pay the interest on the bonds. So they persuaded the government to introduce income taxes, first as a temporary measure, but later permanently, so that it would be able to meet its obligations to the bondholders. In fiscal year 2005, total individual income taxes in the U.S. totalled $927 billion. Of that amount $352 billion, or 38%, was required just to pay interest on the federal debt.

The figure would be higher now. The tragedy is that probably not one cent of that $352 billion was necessary.

It wasn't long after the ink had dried on the Federal Reserve Act before the banksters, as they are often called by people who really understand how the banking system works, decided that an independent press might catch on to the chicanery. Oscar Calloway, is reported in the Congressional Record of February 9, 1917, as follows.

> In March 1915, the J.P. Morgan interests, the steel, shipbuilding, and powder interests, and their subsidiary organizations, got together twelve men high up in the newspaper world, and employed them to select the most influential newspapers in the United States and a sufficient number of them to control generally the policy of the daily press of the United States.... They found it was only necessary to purchase the control of 25 of the greatest papers. The 25 papers were agreed upon; emissaries were sent to purchase the policy, national and international, of these papers; ... an editor was furnished for each paper to properly supervise and edit information regarding the questions of preparedness, militarism, financial policies, and other things of a national and international nature considered vital to the interests of the purchasers [and to suppress] everything in opposition to the wishes of the interests served."[4]

WARS BENEFIT BANKS

World War I was a boon for the banking interests which created tons of money in exchange for government bonds. When the war was over, the money supply was great enough to sustain the house of cards and create a credit bubble which burst in 1929. Sadly, it was Wall Street insiders who inserted the needle after ensuring that they would emerge from the disaster with their wealth intact, and their power enhanced. Seldom in history have an elite few been able to inflict so much pain and misery on millions of innocents.

To make matters worse, the Fed adopted policies that lengthened and deepened the extent of the crisis. I agree with the observation Milton Friedman and Anna Jacobson Schwartz made in their epic *A Monetary History of the United States, 1867-1960*.[5]

When the Federal Reserve Banks closed their doors on March 4, 1933, "The central banking system, set up primarily to render impossible the restrictions of payments by commercial banks, itself joined the commercial banks in a more widespread, complete, and economically disturbing restriction of payments than had ever been experienced in the history of the country. One can certainly sympathize with [President] Hoover's comment about the episode: 'I concluded [the Reserve Board] was indeed a weak reed for a nation to lean on in time of trouble.' "[6] Not only has there been little change in attitude since the 1930s, it appears that little has been learned from the experience. Americans still put their trust in a system regulated by a Fed which gives the interests of the banks and the money-lenders a higher priority than the interests of the country.

Admittedly, the Fed, like most central banks, provided some assistance in helping to provide low-cost money for use by the federal government in financing World War II. Soon after the war, after a successful battle with President Truman, it reverted to its policy of serving the interests of the descendants of the families responsible for its birth, to the near total exclusion of the average American.

Worse, it officially adopted the policies of Milton Friedman and his colleagues at the University of Chicago, and became an active participant in the monetarist revolution. This was mandated by the Policy Committee of the Bank for International Settlements in 1974 with the active support of Fed Chairman Paul Volcker, a disciple of the Nobel Laureate and his philosophy of a self-regulating banking system in which governments would play no part. It proved to be one of the most disastrous ideas in the history of economics.

THE FED – A LAW UNTO ITSELF

When I read that the Fed had never been properly audited I thought of that Biblical adage about "the sins of the fathers being visited on future generations." That certainly is true of the Federal Reserve Act adopted in 1913. The Congress of that year licenced a handful of the richest people in the world to rob the workers of America of a significant slice of their salaries and wages, and to do so silently without sirens screaming, and guns blazing as might happen if any one of us was foolish enough to try robbing a bank.

We, on the other hand, are robbed by people trained as magicians capable of taking money out of our pockets without a real awareness of what is happening to us. In Canada we know, if only after the fact, what our central bank is doing to us. The Bank of Canada, which is 100% owned by Canadian taxpayers, must keep proper accounts, have its books audited by an accredited firm, and make the results available for anyone to see. The Fed has long operated under the conjurer's cloak.

It required a lifetime campaign by former Congressman Ron Paul, who made the unwarranted power and secrecy of the Federal Reserve his passion from the 1970s until it finally became a national issue, to peel the first layer from the veil of secrecy. His stubborn insistence that the public had the right to know how much their currency was being diluted, and who was benefiting from it, finally paid off despite the opposition of Ben Bernanke, Alan Greenspan and various other bankers who vehemently opposed the audit and lied to Congress about the effects an audit would have on markets. Nevertheless, the results of the first audit in the Federal Reserve's 100-year history were posted on Senator Bernie Sanders' webpage on Saturday, September 1, 2012. The story as reported in *Before Its News*, reads as follows:[7]

"What was revealed in the audit was startling:

"$16,000,000,000,000.00 had been secretly given out to US banks and corporations and foreign banks everywhere from France to Scotland. For the period between December 2007 and June 2010, the Federal Reserve had secretly bailed out many of the world's banks, corporations, and governments. The Fed likes to refer to these secret bailouts as an all-inclusive loan program, but virtually none of the money has been returned and it was loaned out at 0% interest. The reasons why the Federal Reserve had never gone public about this, or even informed the United States Congress concerning the $16 trillion dollar bailout is obvious – the American public would have been outraged to find out that the Federal Reserve bailed out foreign banks while Americans were struggling to find jobs.

"To place $16 trillion into perspective, remember that the GDP of the United States was only $16.77 trillion in 2013. The entire national debt of the United States spanning its 200+ years' history was $19.3 trillion. The latest budget to be debated so vigorously in 2015 was $3.8 trillion and the deficit was $43.5 billion – lower than the year before. So it seems incongruous that there was no debate whether or not $16,000,000,000,000 would be given to failing banks and failing corporations around the world.

"In late 2008, the TARP Bailout bill was passed and loans of $800 million were given to failing banks and companies. That was a blatant deception considering the fact that Goldman Sachs alone received 814 billion dollars. As it turns out, the Federal Reserve donated $2.5 trillion to Citigroup, while Morgan Stanley received $2.04 trillion. The Royal Bank of Scotland and Deutsche Bank, a German bank, split about a trillion and numerous other banks received hefty chunks of the $16 trillion.

'This is a clear case of socialism for the rich and rugged, you're-on-your-own individualism for everyone else.' Bernie Sanders (Independent, Vermont)

"When you have conservative Republican stalwarts like Jim Demint (South Carolina) and Ron Paul (Texas) as well as self-identified Democratic socialists like Bernie Sanders all fighting against the Federal Reserve, you know that it is no longer an issue of Right versus Left. When you have every single member of the Republican Party in Congress and a progressive Congressman like Dennis Kucinich sponsoring a bill to audit the Federal Reserve, you realize that the Federal Reserve is an entity unto itself, which has no oversight and no accountability."

AN INCREDIBLE STORY OF INSIDER BAILOUTS

Americans should be swelled with anger and outrage at the abysmal state of affairs when an unelected group of bankers can create money out of thin air and give it out to megabanks and supercorporations like Halloween candy. If the Federal Reserve and the bankers who control it, believe that they can continue to devalue the savings of Americans and to destroy the US economy, they will have to face the realization that their trillion dollar printing presses will eventually plunder the world economy.

The list of institutions that received the most money from the Federal Reserve can be found on page 131 of the GAO Audit and are as follows:

Citigroup: **$2.5 trillion** ($2,500,000,000,000)
Morgan Stanley: **$2.04 trillion** ($2,040,000,000,000)
Merrill Lynch: **$1.949 trillion** ($1,949,000,000,000)
Bank of America: **$1.344 trillion** ($1,344,000,000,000)
Barclays PLC (United Kingdom): **$868 billion** ($868,000,000,000)
Bear Sterns: **$853 billion** ($853,000,000,000)
Goldman Sachs: **$814 billion** ($814,000,000,000)
Royal Bank of Scotland (UK): **$541 billion** ($541,000,000,000)
JP Morgan Chase: **$391 billion** ($391,000,000,000)
Deutsche Bank (Germany): **$354 billion** ($354,000,000,000)
UBS (Switzerland): **$287 billion** ($287,000,000,000)
Credit Suisse (Switzerland): **$262 billion** ($262,000,000,000)
Lehman Brothers: **$183 billion** ($183,000,000,000)
Bank of Scotland (United Kingdom): **$181 billion** ($181,000,000,000)
BNP Paribas (France): **$175 billion** ($175,000,000,000)

And many many more including banks in Belgium of all places.

(Google: Government Accountability Office, audit of the Federal Reserve, July 21, 2011 to read the 266-page report.)

The list goes on and on!

Wow! Aren't these figures enough to rock your socks? Imagine the Fed diluting the money supply by trillions and without any authority other than its own. The Congress and, as far as we know, the White House, were kept completely in the dark.

THE FED AND THE CORONAVIRUS PANDEMIC

Just as the Fed had come to the aid of the Administration in World War II, it was required to do so again when the Coronavirus Pandemic struck. It was a war of a very different kind, but there were similarities as well.

The financial bubble had burst, and there was a shortage of cash everywhere. The value of securities listed on the New York Stock Exchange fell about 30 percent in a few days. Banks with huge portfolios were in real trouble. Much worse were the situations of individuals who lost their jobs, small businesses that had to close temporarily, and revenues lost by governments at all levels. There was no denying a crisis of major proportions.

Then a small miracle happened. The Fed agreed to work in harmony with the Treasury. To quote Ellen Brown, one of the few people I know who understands the ins and outs of the financial labyrinth, "It took only a few days for Congress to unanimously pass the Coronavirus Aid Relief, and Economic Security (CARES Act), which will be doling out $2.3 trillion in crisis relief, most of it going to Corporate America with few strings attached."[8] There were other provisions of significance.

But there was self-serving on the part of the Fed when it departed from its vaunted policy of "Independence". "It needed the Treasury to help it bail out a financial industry burdened with an avalanche of dodgy assets that are fast losing value. The problem for the Fed is that it is only allowed to purchase or lend against securities with government guarantees, including Treasury securities, etc."[9]

So the incentive was to preserve some of the Rothschild's vast holdings. They are the controlling interest in the Fed and would not allow the people to claim it without a bigger fight. So who are these people who call themselves the Rothschilds?

BALTIC TRIBES
URALIC TRIBES
VOLGA BULGARIAN KHANATE
KIMAK KHANATES
BURTAS
BASHKIRS
EAST SLAVS
WEST SLAVS
MAGYARS
KARLUKS
Kiev (Sambat)
Atil-Khazaran
KHAZARIA
PECHENEGS
DANUBE BULGARIAN KHANATE
Kerch
Gusliyev
Samandar
Tamatarkha
Khersones
Sudak
Balanjar
ABKHAZIA
ALANIA
Pliska
GEORGIA
Derbent
OGHUZ TURKS
Adrianople
Sinope
Constantinople
KHAZAR (CASPIAN) SEA
Trebizond
Tfilis
HUNS
Thessalonika
Nikomedia
ARMENIA
Urgench
BYZANTINE EMPIRE
Nikaea
Ancyra
Sabastaea
Baku
Smyrna
Ephesus
Merv
Athens
Tarsus
Edessa
Tabriz
Rayy
Antioch
Aleppo
Mosul
Kirkuk
Mashdad
ABBASID CALIPHATE
Tyre
Damascus
Baghdad
Kermanshah
Isfahan
Jaffa
ABBASID CALIPHATE
Yazd
Alexandria
Jerusalem
Basra
Kerman

CHAPTER TEN

THE KAZARIAN CONNECTION

"I didn't know how much I didn't know because I didn't know how much there was to know."

– Paul Hellyer

I must admit that until about three years ago I had never heard of the ancient land of Khazaria. It was news to me. I would guess that the vast majority of my readers have been equally uninformed. No one knew where Khazaria was located geographically. One of my erudite readers came to the rescue by suggesting that the kingdom comprised the regions of southern Russia, northern Caucasus, eastern Ukraine, Crimea, western Kazakhstan and northwestern Uzbekistan.

The Khazarians apparently became known as a dangerous race for visitors and travellers passing through their territory. Robbery was commonplace and, from time to time, tourists were murdered, and their identities stolen. The situation was so bad that around 800 AD the leaders of the surrounding nations, especially Russia, responded to the many complaints by sending an ultimatum to the Khazarian King.

The King was given an option to choose one of the three Abrahamic religions, Islam, Christianity or Judaism and make it his official state religion and require all Khazarian citizens to practice it, including the children. The King chose Judaism and promised to stay within the requirements laid out by the surrounding confederacy of nations led by the Russian czar. Despite his promise the King and the inner circle of oligarchs continue practicing their centuries old customs, including their evil ways.

Eventually Russia and the surrounding nations had had enough and they invaded Khazaria. But the King's spies knew in advance that the attack was coming; so they escaped to European nations to the West taking their vast fortune of gold and silver with them. They wisely changed their identities to prevent being pursued in their new country of choice. At the same time they swore an oath that no matter how long it took they would one day take their revenge against the Russians.[1]

THE ROTHSCHILD FAMILY

Quite a few of the Khazars settled in Germany where they had the opportunity to pursue their skills and interests. It appears from the available information that one of these families were the Bauers. They were experienced bankers and they prospered in their new environment, and eventually changed their name to Rothschild. The name is derived from the German "zum rothen schild (with the old spelling "ch", meaning "at the red shield," in the house where the family lived for many generations.)[2]

One of my favourite childhood memories was watching a movie about the Rothschild family. The scene I remember best was one of the family sitting down to a sumptuous dinner with a roast of either turkey or goose about to be carved and, if I remember correctly, one or more wine bottles on the table along with the other elements of a family feast.

There was a knock on the door that was assumed to be that of a tax collector. "Just a minute please," was the response. Immediately, with military efficiency, everything disappeared into large wooden bread boxes and nothing remained on the table except bread. The door was opened, the taxman took a quick look around, and then left apparently convinced that it was just a poor family having dinner. I have no way of knowing whether the portrayal was fact or fiction but I got the impression that there might be future occasions when reports were filed on the basis of incomplete information.

Wikipedia says that "during the 19th century, the Rothschild family possessed the largest private fortune in the world, as well as in modern world history."[3] There is no doubting that. It then goes on to suggest "the family's wealth declined over the 20th century ..."[4] That statement is not credible! Speaking as one who has kept a watchful eye on the financial world I can say that the Rothschild Family Dynasty has been, and continues to be the wealthiest of the wealthy world elite. The only one capable of keeping its name off the Forbes list of the world's wealthiest people. It is also the world's most powerful force, more so than any U.S. president.

It is also fair to say that the Rothschild family didn't achieve that unique position by observing the ten commandments set out in the Jewish and Christian Bibles, or by adhering to the laws of Moses as relayed to the Jewish people on behalf of the Creator God. They acquired their unique and incalculable wealth by a combination of absolute secrecy and making their own rules of conduct designed to favor their own self-interest.

When chapter six related the many ways in which the Bank for International Settlements aided the German Nazis before, during and after World War II there was no mention of the Rothschilds name. Similarly with the Basel agreements I, II and III. They should be called the Rothschild Rules, because you can be sure that they were either written or approved by the Rothschilds before the Basel label was attached.

THE STATE OF ISRAEL

One of the Rothschild family's proudest achievements was the establishment of the modern state of Israel on May 14th 1948. They provided much of the money and the political clout to achieve United Nations approval of a demarcation line that gave the new state the lion's share of what had been Palestine. There was considerable sympathy for the idea of a safe haven for survivors of the Holocaust and other homeless Jews.

That initial sympathy was eroded over time as the Israelis made it clear that their hopes and aims included annexing ever more of the small remnant that was Palestine, and the only hope for an independent land of their own for the sons and daughters of Abraham and Ismael. To this end the Israelis, who were supposed to be the Palestinians blood brothers, treated them abominably and certainly not in accordance with the Torah.

The inconsistencies of the situation are beginning to come to light. Why would a family with deep roots in the Nazi party sponsor a safe haven for the few Abrahamic Jews who escaped indescribably evil Nazis? And why would the longtime Israeli Prime Minister Benjamin Netanyahu supply a secret Nazi group in Germany with atomic weapons in exchange for missile-firing submarines? The only rational answer is that modern Israel was intended as the first land grab toward the ultimate establishment of a new Khazarian Empire.

Meanwhile the Rothschild Blitzkrieg continues. Following World War II they were key players in the formation of the Bilderberg Group. This highly secretive organization which includes the banking cartel, has been at the apex of the Cabal that has been engineering the New World Order. The NWO is the cover code for a fascist world government decades in the making.

David Rockefeller was in from the beginning and, as he bragged in his *Memoirs* quoted earlier, was very proud of the progress that the Bilderbergers had made toward a new world government of "bankers and the elite." According to Ellen Hodgson Brown, Rockefeller became " webmaster" for the bankers after World War II.

This was a big shift from the Rockefeller tradition. His father, John D. Rockefeller, was a life-long Christian who paid for the construction of Park Avenue Baptist Church in New York City (now Central Presbyterian Church). Some cynics say John D. was the kind of Christian who prayed on his knees on Sunday, and preyed on the people the other six days of the week. In any event John D. arranged for the Rockefeller Foundation to make large annual donations to the church for its continued operations. Some years ago these payments ended because, as the minister told me personally, the boys (Rockefeller Brothers) have other interests.[5] On the basis of information that I have on the roles of the Bilderbergers and the Cabal it is easy to conclude that it was not just a change in interest but a change in allegiance from nominal Christianity to Luciferianism AKA Satanism. If the age old axiom "people are known by the company they keep" has any validity, the evidence is overwhelming.

I have learned a great deal in the course of researching and writing this book. For example, the Nazi base in Antarctica was not begun when they realized that they could not win the war. It was launched much earlier and was under construction from about the time the war started. It had progressed to the point where it was able to defeat Admiral Byrd's expedition, and then to send an enlarged Hannebu III spacecraft that carried a large crew to officially establish the German Mars colony in mid January 1946.[6]

THE FOURTH REICH

Today it's Aries Prime facility consists of three separate Martian bases that are all connected underground.[7] There is constant traffic between the Mars establishment and Base 211, as the Antarctica base has been named. The third member of the triumvirate that comprises the Fourth Reich is the eight-storey headquarters on the dark side of our moon that Len Kasten describes as their equivalent of the U.S. Pentagon.[8]

All three bases are controlled by the Nazi-Reptilian partnership that is strongly backed by the Dracos, the number one enemy of the Galactic Federation of Light (one of its names) comprising those species and civilizations that are loyal to the Creator God of Heaven and Earth. According to some informants, the two groups, the Federation of Light on behalf of the Creator God, and the Draconian Empire comprised primarily of Reptilians and some Grays, loyal to God's errant son Lucifer, have been fighting over control of our solar system for thousands of years.

It is not surprising that the two groups are as different as night and day, or evil and good. Representatives of the Federation are kind, caring and compassionate. They are anxious to help us humans. The mind-controlled Nazis, on the other hand, have a total disregard for those of the human species that are not one of them. Their record of behaviour in World War II was absolutely despicable.

In two of Len Kasten's books he reviews the Nazi atrocities in detail. For many of us the level of savagery is almost beyond belief. Humans were treated as slaves. They were overworked and undernourished. If they failed to meet quotas some were starved to death and others shot. Some of Germany's best-known industries were similarly intolerant towards their slave labour.

Regrettably the Fourth Reich appears to be as ruthless as the Third Reich was. Nearly all of their slave labour is kidnapped. Kasten tells us the story of CIA involvement in abducting children to be raised as slaves. It is so horrible that I won't repeat it here; but it does confirm my recommendation that the CIA be shut down at once. The army should occupy Langley and turn it into a library-museum for truth-seeking researchers.

THE NAZI INFLUENCE IN AMERICA

The Nazi plan for planet Earth is one of their most highly classified secrets. Still they have telegraphed their intention to establish an unelected government, a new world order (NWO) that would be fascist (Nazi) in nature. In addition their plan for a dramatic reduction in Earth's population was reported by whistleblower Phil Schneider, who had worked with them underground helping them build cities, before he allegedly committed suicide. (The fact that it was recorded as a suicide convinces me that the U.S. justice system is totally corrupt.)

German scientists brought to the U.S. under Operation Paperclip immediately after World War II, to assist in the fight against the Soviets, have been involved in the American Space Program almost from the beginning. One of the flying saucers that crashed near Roswell, New Mexico, in 1947, was back engineered by American and Nazi scientists who moved the operation to Nevada, where it would be inaccessible to both U.S. government and the press.

The progress that has been made on the technical side in the intervening decades is absolutely amazing. So is the success that the Cabal and the Bilderbergers have had in keeping the project totally secret from the public and the Congress.

Only recently has the flood of credible evidence begun. One of the most dramatic is the following revelation emailed to a list of friends by Richard Boylan PhD., concerning the Nautilus spaceship.

"The Nautilus, the Earth's only Interstellar deep space ship, (shown here in rough illustration; real Nautilus photos not available). The actual Nautilus, an enormous metallic cylindrical vessel is about a half-mile long, and as wide as three football fields end-to-end. It is operated by NASA, is forbidden for warfare and only for peaceful uses, has an international crew, and only undertakes a visit to other solar systems with explicit prior permission of Star Nations Organization, our Milky Way Galaxy's official government.

The Nautilus is a classified fully anti-gravity spaceship, built for deep space travel. It is the only one of the twelve U.S. antigravity craft engineered to be able to leave the solar system and travel to the stars. The Nautilus's Deep Space capability is what Dr. Ben Rich, the head of Lockheed-Martin's Advanced-Projects 'Skunk Works' was referring to in a 1993 speech to UCLA alumni when he stated, 'we already have the means to travel among the stars, but these technologies are locked up in black projects.' The Nautilus is shaped like a stubby metallic cylinder, somewhat like a short silver cigar 1000 yards long by 300 yards in diameter. with its interstellar travel technology, the Nautilus is extremely expensive to manufacture. $870 billion per copy. thus far only four have been built. The Nautilus is manufactured jointly by Boeing Phantom Works, Lockheed-Martin's Advanced Development Program, and Airbus Industries Anglo-French-EU Consortium, and assembled at the sprawling underground facilities of the Nevada National Security Site west of Area 51, Nevada. A retired top Boeing executive confirmed to Dr. Boylan that Boeing's Phantom Works had teamed up with Europe's Airbus Industries to help manufacture the Nautilus secret spaceship. The Nautilus operates clandestinely out of underground hangars east of Niland, California under Black Peak on the restricted Marine Corps/Navy's Chocolate Mountain Aerial Gunnery Range east of the Salton Sea. Unlike other anti-gravity craft, the Nautilus is not operated by the military but by the NASA-ESA Consortium, and is reserved for peaceful uses only."[9]

The U.S. Armed Forces have also spent these many decades designing and developing a military space Fleet described as Solar Warden.[10] It is extremely well advanced and includes support activities at a number of celestial locations. It was long assumed that the fleet would be used as a false flag operation to frighten us, and persuade us to accept martial law without resistance. This fleet, however, has a capability far greater than would be required for a fly by.

There are thousands of loyal and patriotic Americans but there are very few who know what has been going on for the last 70 years as the Nazis transformed their beautiful country into a police state. In 2013 I was one of 40 witnesses at a Citizen Hearing on Disclosure, organized by Steve Bassett, Paradigm Research Group, April 29th to May 3rd. The format was to have five former Congressmen and Congresswomen, and one former U.S. Senator, act as a mock Congressional Committee hearing. Not one of the six had ever heard of a UFO, even though at that time the U.S. had a Space Fleet and trillions of dollars had been spent on it.

So the degree of naivety was and remains so great that the Nazi-controlled government can get away with murder, probably literally. The ruling Cabal still comprises members of the Bavarian Illuminati, almost certainly Khazarians who hate the Russians with a burning hate, and the Nazis who comprise the majority of the military junta, who hate both the Russians and the Americans for entering World War II on the side of the Allies, that sealed their fate.

So the United States, and a considerable part of the Western World, are like a civilization sitting on the top of an active volcano that may or may not erupt, depending on events yet to be born. It may be possible to defund and defang the madmen, but it will require a mass mobilization to do it.

THE FINAL STRAWS

There are usually one or two acts in a long series of unhappy events which Trigger action that has been considered or contemplated for a long time. One speculative event and another that is ironclad should do it. They both relate to the international banking cartel. I read an email from a Republican candidate for the U.S. Senate, in the November 2020 election, accusing the banksters of using the Coronavirus to crash the economic system to their considerable financial benefit. Is that true? I don't know. There was a rumour beginning in January 2020 that the banking cartel would crash the system in the spring. Also, there is an old axiom of "follow the money." The poor and small business owners will suffer dramatically, if not desperately from the Coronavirus Pandemic, while the elite bankers will profit to the tune of billions if not trillions of dollars.

THE TRUTH MAY NEVER BE KNOWN

The next is the final, final straw. The article is headed: "Catherine Austin Fitts - We Are Watching The Mother Of All Debt Entrapments."[11] The following are just a few important paragraphs from an article you can find on the internet.

"Former assistant housing secretary and publisher of the Solari report, Catherine Austin Fitts joins Greg Hunter to talk about her latest report, entitled 'The Injection Fraud' about the massive vaccine gambit currently in play and how this is a vital part of the central bankers' 'global reset.'

"THE GLOBAL RESET

"So, what we are seeing is a re-engineering of the global financial system and governance system, 'Just Do It' method and of course, a very important part of that is we see a lot of smart money get out of the market in the top of January, in February and then March, a push to basically use police powers created through the healthcare system, to shut down a huge part of the independent economy, globally.

"So, small business, small farms shut down across the board, throwing both the emerging markets and many small businesses into debt traps. So, we are watching the mother of all debt entrapment going on globally and that means we're in for a very radical re-engineering and of course, that's what we're seeing in the US.

"You can cut out a lot of overhead and basically have everybody ... on the system and that's why I keep saying, crypto is not a currency. It's the end of currencies. But you're talking about an all digital system, where they can turn your money off and on. You know what this is called, if you're a Christian. It's called the Mark of the Beast. That's what they are trying to do here."[12]

I say that enough is enough. The reign of the corrupt banksters must end now. So the answer to this latest proposal of entrapment is no! No! No! No! Debt slavery must end once and for all time. Liberation lies in seizing the Fed and all of its subsidiaries and adopting the liberating package set out in the next chapter.

CHAPTER ELEVEN

THE SOLUTIONS

"Nothing is more powerful than an idea whose time has come."
–Victor Hugo

Wow! Do we have work to do!

But don't lose heart. Remember the former baseball player, Yogi Berra, who said "The game isn't over, 'til its over." It can be won by millions of decent Americans deciding that it would be better to use their people power to thwart the plans of the Khazarians and the Nazis than to die at their hands.

The Congress has the power to reverse the course of history if it can be persuaded to use it. The weapon of choice is money. It should reduce defense expenditures by 50 percent to bring them back in line with what they were before Bibi Netanyahu and the Mossad decided to attack the United States on September 11ᵗʰ, 2001, in the premeditated crime of the century. Perhaps Netanyahu and the head of the Mossad at the time should be extradited to stand trial in the U.S.

The defense cuts have to be directed to achieve specific goals.

THE NATIONAL SECURITY AGENCY (NSA)

The National Security Agency (NSA) should be shut down at once, but only on an interim basis until the war is over. Putting the massive spy agency in mothballs will level the playing field and make it impossible for the Nazis to know who among their numbers has opted to tell the truth and who has not. At least the massive spying organization will become inert until the situation has become sufficiently stabilized, that the Congress can decide how much universal spying should end, and how many selective targets, if any, remain.

THE DEFENSE ADVANCED RESEARCH PROJECTS AGENCY (DARPA)

The Defense Advanced Research Projects Agency (DARPA) should be completely shut down until the Congress can examine and review all of its advanced projects from a moral and ethical point of view. Is DAR-

PA involved in experiments to develop beings that are half human and half machine? If so what is the purpose of its experiments, and is it one that our Creator God would approve?

CHEMTRAILS, HAARP AND AN IONIZED SKY

The U.S. President should order the armed forces to cease and desist from using chemtrails-HAARP and an ionized sky, this most evil of projects. In one fell swoop he would eliminate their ability to use weather as a weapon. Global warming is creating more than enough extreme variations in weather patterns without adding to it artificially.

The chemtrail-HAARP ionized fence has been designed to encourage psychotic generals into believing that the U.S. could wage a nuclear war with Russia and suffer only acceptable casualties. This is sheer madness, of course, but when generals are subject to mind control they cease to be rational. This same "fence" is designed to discourage any good ETs who might consider coming to our rescue from doing so.

Finally, Phil Schneider was correct when he said that part of the Cabal agenda is a drastic reduction in the world's population. The fascists would only have to insert a lethal virus in their chemtrail mix to kill millions of people within 48 hours. So those countries, including Canada, who have been duped into believing that the chemtrails are related to climate control, I say tear up your agreement with the U.S. and act immediately. No need for studies or commissions of inquiry, the health and possibly the lives of your citizens are in danger until you end this horrific system.

GROUND THE SPACE FORCE

The U.S. President should issue an order grounding all space vehicles of every kind until the question of who will represent the Earth in space has been agreed by all the major powers, including Russia and China in particular. Another arms race is inevitable in the absence of a diplomatic solution, which must become the norm.

Certainly the Nazi-controlled U.S. fleet should sit on the ground until all crews have been screened for allegiance to the U.S. constitution and the people of America. Space travel offers an exciting new frontier, but we are not welcome into deep space until we abandon our frontier mentality of shoot first and ask questions after, which has been our *modus vivendi* until now.

For many years Dr. Stephen Greer, M.D., one of the world's foremost ufologists, has been warning that the Space Command, now the Space

Force, is planning the final False Flag attack in the Cabal's plan to take over the world.[1] Dr. Greer has literally put his life on the line for saying this. But isn't it the truth?

At the Alien Cosmic Exhibition in Toronto, in Sept. 2019, a representative of the U.S. Armed Forces, Randy Kramer, said that there would be an attack (on Earth?) in 18 to 24 months. He couldn't possibly know that if it was to be an Alien attack. His knowledge would be limited to what the U.S. Space Force planned to do.[2]

THE CENTRAL INTELLIGENCE AGENCY

The CIA is near the top of the list of "An Action Plan for Americans to Take Back Control of America." When I think of the CIA I am reminded of Baron Josiah Stamp's description of the Bank of England of which he was a director from 1928-1941. He said: "Banking was conceived in inequity and was born in sin."

I would say the same was true of the CIA. The whole idea of fighting a worldwide clandestine war to impose the ill-defined ideological precepts of a single country is anathema to our God-given freedom of choice. Worse, such a war was doomed from its inception. Tim Weiner's monumental book. *Legacy of Ashes*, tells the story.

To paraphrase Sir Winston Churchill you might conclude that never in the annals of human history have so many people spent so much time and tax payers' money in illegal acts of bribery, murder, mayhem, political interference on behalf of the candidate of choice, the undermining of democratically elected leaders and myriad other misdemeanours outside the law with so little positive and lasting results to show for it.

The CIA introduced torture, which is one of Satan's tools. It has promoted the policy of continual war. It has also, according to various accounts, been one of the biggest, if not the biggest, drug dealer in America, despite the U.S. war against drugs. I listened to a YouTube session describing the CIA importing drugs in the bodies of dead service men. Also, not long ago, I had a long chat with a former USAF F104 pilot who flew as escort for a CIA Dreamlifter cargo plane filled with drugs. How many young lives have been ruined by using the drugs the CIA has been peddling to raise money for its Black Operations?[3]

The CIA should be locked and shuttered at once and there should be a lengthy jail term for anyone who either shreds or removes documents of any kind.

THE MONEY MONOPOLY

All of the above actions are essential to begin the process of stabilization in what has become an extremely volatile situation. There is one more critically important action without which the plan will fail. The Rothschild domination of the world banking and financial system must end. The Fed has to be seized, converted into a publicly owned Bank of the United States, and cash reserves have to be re-instated for all banks to the point where recessions and depressions will be no more!

THE THREE MYTHS OF MONEY

1. Money is real and has intrinsic value. That is not true! Money has no intrinsic value except for old or commemorative coins minted with precious metals. Graham Towers, the first, and in my opinion the best of Governors or equivalent, said: "Money is just a book entry. That's all it is." If he were alive today he would say, "Money is just a computer entry. That's all it is."

2. The money you borrow from your bank is money that someone else deposited a few days or weeks earlier. Although that is theoretically possible, the odds of it happening are infinitesimal. The money the bank lends to you is created out of thin air (by a tap on a computer) just for you. When you pay off a loan the money disappears back into thin air, and the collateral you provided to obtain the loan is returned.

3. Central bankers know best, and we should accept their judgement. If you track their record for the last century or so you will arrive at the opposite conclusion. They have caused more pain and grief than any group on Earth with the possible exception of the economists whose advise they have adopted.

ISSUES TO BE ADDRESSED

There are a number of issues that have to be addressed in addition to putting an end to the Rothschild control of the banking industry, and through it much of the world. At the top of the list is the restoration of democracy. For years most Western countries have not been masters of their own destiny. They have called themselves democracies but that has been a misnomer. Consequently, government of by and for the people should be near the top of the list.

Another criteria that I consider important is a smooth transition. The knots in the financial rope have to be eliminated one at a time. Meanwhile governments at all levels should have access to enough money to balance their budgets at all levels without borrowing. This should be true in both substance and cosmetics. The money governments create for themselves should, for all intents and purposes, be debt free.

The mechanics that my colleagues and I devised is a very simple one. When governments take money from their own central bank they should just print non-transferable, non-convertible, non-redeemable share certificates in the U.S., Canada, the U.K. or any country creating money. These shares are the collateral the central banks needs to balance their books. The system has become too complicated to just have the Treasury Department print bills. Therefore leave the functions in the hands of the central bank and provide it with shares instead of bonds equal to the cash created. Thomas Edison said "any country whose credit is good enough to issue a bond, is good enough to issue a bill." I agree!

There are two objectives, one short term and one long term. Most governments need very large amounts of cash to recover from the devastating consequences of the Coronavirus Pandemic, in addition to years of austerity budgeting that has left many essential services with inadequate funds to do their jobs well, let alone to modernize.

We are recommending the creation of an amount of cash equal to five percent of the total bank deposits. This would be repeated for seven years or until private banks have accumulated cash reserves of 34% of their deposits. This time frame is long enough that governments at all levels will know that they can undertake major projects and have funds guaranteed to complete them.

At the end of the seven years governments will create 34% of the increase in the money supply each year which should be sufficient for balanced budgets at the federal, state and municipal levels at existing or lower tax levels. In some cases there should be surpluses that could be used for debt reductions.

Of course federal governments would have the power to monetize debt, but I would urge them to be prudent and not rock the boat. There are insurance companies, savings funds of various kinds and individuals who rely on government bonds for investment. So their needs have to be accommodated.

I should also make it clear that there are other groups of monetary reformers whose ideas are admirable. I spoke to the "Positive Money" group in England, and I know many disciples of Modern Monetary Theory (MMT). A few years ago I would have been content with just injecting government-created money into the system. But now I know that the issues are much larger and more complex than I would have dreamed at that time. So I and my colleagues had to adjust accordingly.

I have chosen three examples to illustrate the recommended approach, the United States, the United Kingdom, and Canada. If my information is correct, the U.K. bought the Bank of England after World War II, when the Rothschild Interest was nationalized, though their ideas linger on.

The Bank of Canada was chartered in 1934 as a private company in which several banks had significant interests. The Canadian Prime Minister, William Lyon Mackenzie King nationalized the bank in 1938 at the suggestion of one enlightened monetary reformer, Gerry McGeer, M.P. All of the shares are now owned by the Minister of Finance on behalf of the Canadian people.

The United States must seize complete control of The Federal Reserve System and charter a new Bank of the United States by an Act of Congress. I don't think my American cousins could do better than use the Bank of Canada Act as an easy guide to adapt to U.S. circumstances. The one addition, which will also have to be inserted in the Canadian document, is a clause to make non-transferable, non-convertible, non-redeemable shares in the United States of America acceptable collateral for the creation of currency.

It may also be necessary to make any amendments necessary to require U.S. banks to acquire cash reserves against their deposits at the rate of not less than 5% per annum until a level of 34% has been established. This will ensure that there will be no inflation from the government-created money.

In the event of a disagreement between the Governor of the Bank of the United States and the Secretary of the Treasury in respect of the amount by which the money supply should be increased, or the rate of interest for overnight lending, the view of the Secretary shall prevail. In any such case, however, the direction of the Secretary shall be made public forthwith. This procedure is consistent with the principles of democracy, and should eliminate future cases of monetary and fiscal policies being at odds, rather than working in harmony. Here are the figures for the three countries.

Month of March 2020		
Country	Total Deposits	5% of Total Deposits
Canada ($USD)*	$3,261,144,000,000.00	$163,057,200,000.00
U.S. ($USD)**	$14,742,490,000,000.00	$737,124,500,000.00
U.K. ($USD)***	$3,768,552,000,000.00	$188,427,600,000.00
Canada ($CAD)****	$4,550,274,223,200.00	$227,513,711,160.00

*	https://www.ceicdata.com/en/indicator/canada/total-deposits
**	https://www.ceicdata.com/en/indicator/united-states/total-deposits
***	https://www.ceicdata.com/en/indicator/united-kingdom/total-deposits
	USD to CAD, Mar 2020 - **1.3953**
	Monthly Avg. Exchange rate from Bank of Canada
****	https://www.bankofcanada.ca/rates/exchange/monthly-exchange-rates/

Our earlier recommendation for Canada was that the share certificates be given a nominal value of $10 billion each. For the U.S. a combination of $50 billion and $10 billion denominations would make more sense. Also there is no reason the numbers involved can't be rounded out. Contrary to some observers and academics, economics is not an exact science. It should be called political-economy, as it was when I was a young man.

The U.S. figure seems too low for me even if they all come from the same source. I would round it out at a trillion dollars to be divided 50% to the federal government, 25% to the various states in proportion to their population, and 25% to the municipalities on the same basis. The objective is to get a system that works for the people who own the right to create money, while keeping the banking industry alive and useful.

CANADA BLEW IT

The latest two Canadian governments, the first Conservative, and its Liberal successor have both had access to our plan to utilize the publicly owned Bank of Canada to create $150 billion dollars a year of debt-free money (based on the level of bank deposits at the time). Neither had the courtesy to respond. I reminded the present prime minister of the plan in a letter sent the day he took office for the first time, and volunteered to help him put it into effect. There was no response. Instead he adopted classical Keynesianism and stimulated the Canadian economy by putting the country further in debt. It is obvious that neither Prime Minister Justin Trudeau, nor his finance minister Bill Morneau, understand the rudiments of money and banking.

When Elizabeth May, the Leader of the Green Party, filed a written question on the House of Commons Order Paper asking Finance Minister Morneau why he didn't use the Bank of Canada to create money for infrastructure, the minister's simple response was "It would be far too inflationary." That was not the truth, as Table 1 of this book clearly shows.

Instead of using the Bank of Canada creatively, as good Liberal governments did for many years, Minister Morneau opted to set up an Infrastructure Bank. He asked BlackRock, the World's largest financial investment company to help design it. In her amazing book *Beyond Banksters*, Joyce Nelson warns us that this was the first gigantic step down the wrong road for Canadian government finance.[4]

MORE THAN "BAD OPTICS"

In an outrageous display of corporate arrogance, on November 14, 2016 BlackRock hosted a private summit in Toronto for "a select group of major international investors" with trillions of dollars in assets. They were allowed to meet and question PM Trudeau, Finance Minister Bill Morneau, Infrastructure Minister Amarjeet Sohi, and other federal officials, but the press was not allowed to be there to record the "opportunities" that our elected politicians were offering these banksters.[5]

And in the latest move, on March 27 2020— the same day that the U.S. Congress approved the bailout bill making BlackRock a key financial overseer – Canada's publicly-owned central bank, the Bank of Canada (BoC), suddenly announced that BlackRock will act as its advisor for a new quantitative-easing (QE) program for corporations – basically a money-spigot for a struggling corporate sector.

There was no tendering process for this role, and as one financial writer noted, BoC Governor Stephen Poloz appeared to be "opting to put urgency ahead of dithering over potential traps such as conflicts of interest, a rushed tendering process and bad optics." But let's be clear: the central banks on both sides of the Canada-U.S. border have now placed BlackRock in a primary position for effecting monetary and fiscal policy in both countries. That is much more than "bad optics". That is flagrant corporatism.

MORE OF THE SAME OLD SAME OLD

Whenever I read about BlackRock and Larry Fink my mind turns toward the Rothschilds, and what I believe to be the inevitable connection. Larry Fink was to be aboard to protect and enhance the Rothschild's interests. In the huge payout by the Fed I saw the image of the Rothschilds rescuing the Rothschilds. In the absence of the action I am recommending, I can foresee the escape from the huge financial pit being dug by the Pandemic becoming a bonanza for the Rothschild empire, and an even deeper bondage for the wealth producing people of the world.

An excellent Article by Eric Zuesse is worth quoting – because it underlines the depth of the problem.

> Why Post Coronavirus America will have massive poverty April 22, 2020.
> "America's bailout package to overcome the Coronavirus 'recession' is twofold:
>
> One part is printing money for employees and consumers, so that their investments will still have value and there won't be panicked selling of them as corporations accumulate soaring losses because consumers are staying home and cutting back on expenses.
>
> One part is printing money for employees and consumers, so that they won't be thrown out onto the streets for non-payment of debts such as mortgages, car-loans, credit cards and student loans.
>
> Another part is printing money for bondholders and stockholders, so that their investments will still have value and there won't be panicked selling of them as corporations accumulate soaring losses because consumers are staying home and are cutting way back on expenses.
>
> The top-down part of the bailout (the part for investors) will merely add to the wealth of the already-wealthy, while everybody else sinks financially into oblivion. (On April 9th, the *Zero Hedge* financial site explained in detail why even bailing out the airlines would hurt the economy more than help the economy.) The top-down part supplies the money to the corporations instead of to their employees and consumers, and is therefore supply-boosting instead of demand-boosting. Supplying money to the corporations that the Government selects to protect will enable those corporations to buy up assets and corporations which during the crisis are being auctioned off by the ones that go out of business, and this will leave the nation's wealth in even fewer hands than before the epidemic struck.

The bottom-up part (the part for workers and consumers) will be exactly the opposite of that: it will help prevent another Great Depression. By boosting purchases, instead of bailing-out billionaires and such, it will not increase the concentration of wealth.

However, employees and consumers don't have many lobbyists, but billionaires do, and billionaires also own (through political donations and lobbyists) almost all members of Congress (and also the mainstream press), and they not only own, but are represented by, one inside the White House, who is surrounded there by others, and by representatives of others, so that the concerns of the wealthiest will be very well represented by America's Government, and will end up dominating the bailouts, so that only the insiders, who are well-connected in Washington, will be protected. (And Joe Biden would be no improvement over Donald Trump, though his rhetoric is different.)

Already, we see, in the 'news'-reports, that there is 'chaos' etc. in the U.S. Government's response to the crisis, but what's not being reported in the mainstream 'news'-media is that there very much is method to this seeming madness, and it is the method of the well-practiced and well-funded takers, definitely not of their victims, from whom they (and their Government) have been, and now increasingly are, taking. The takers own the Deep State, and are protected by it. The vast bulk of the bailouts will go to them. The vast bulk of the bailouts will go to the suppliers (investors), not to their worker's and consumers.

So, as a general rule: the more that a person's income depends upon investments, and the less that it depends upon their labour (wages), the more fully that the bailouts will compensate for the losses they'll be suffering as a result of the Coronavirus disruptions."[6]

Zuesse states the case well, we don't need to worry about the billionaires because they have the power and influence to look after themselves. But what about the poor. No-one, especially the billionaires, seems to care about them. This point was engraved indelibly on me as I watched the demonstrations and riots in many U.S. cities at the end May and early June, 2020. The rage was palpable. To me the protesters were saying "nobody cares about me, our jobs, our pay, our dignity and even our lives. But hear us; we are real people with the same hopes and aspirations as other people, and our lives are as valuable as their lives. We, too, are members of the human species and we want to be treated as equals, not serfs.

A GUARANTEED ANNUAL INCOME

The last few weeks, for the first time ever, I have given some serious thought to the concept of a guaranteed annual income. For many years I have promoted the idea of guaranteed annual work. If the private business sector can't provide jobs for the unemployed, the government should. There are many useful things to be done and governments are going to play a much more active role in creating them as the number of unemployed increases, and artificial intelligence (AI) eliminates more and more of the traditional jobs.

The Coronavirus Pandemic has created massive unemployment and one has to wonder how many of those will be gone forever. The daily paper I read has shown pictures of a number of well-known restaurants and bars that have closed forever. I also wonder when, if ever, the thousands of jobs lost in air travel will return. Meanwhile the government of Canada has been doling out cash to millions of unemployed. A new program has been announced every few days but there are still individuals, the self-employed and gig workers who have fallen through the cracks. Governments at all levels are beginning to wonder what comes next. Is there any solution to the mess that has been created in good faith?

I have sometimes fancied myself as a problem solver. The present challenge, however, is not one that I would want because it is too complicated. It would take a couple of oracles to reconcile so many different programs, and the arbitrary lines drawn between who qualifies and who does not.

The plan my colleagues and I have presented have universal application to alleviate the financial problems of governments at all levels. But what about the poor? They have no guarantees. They will still be dependent on governments capable of confronting everyone with enough red tape to drive a sane person crazy.

The final thrust came after watching the protesters and rioters in various U.S. cities following the murder of George Floyd on May 25, 2020. There was a protest in my city of Toronto as well. Not only are blacks subject to systemic racism, many of them have problems getting jobs except the ones we whites don't want to do. Blacks deserve to be treated with dignity and be recognized as fellow citizens and human beings. So do the aboriginals who have also been mistreated and marginalized for centuries despite the fact that they are the ones who really care about our planetary home, and want to save it for our children and grandchildren as well as their own.

So I have decided to bite the bullet, as the saying goes. Our under-appreciated brothers and sisters want action, so let us seize this golden opportunity to act. A little action is better than a thousand words, and the promises of most politicians.

Of course there will be a few people who take advantage, and don't really try for a real job. But they are a small minority. And who is to say that artists, singers and thinkers don't enrich us more than some billionaires who don't do anything that you could rightly call useful work? A guaranteed annual income will create a modicum of justice!

BITCOINS & CRYPTOCURRENCIES

These two categories are also the products of some imaginative entrepreneur who devise products that can be used to claim goods and services provided by others without themselves contributing any real wealth for the common good. Like the banking Ponzi scheme, they can best be described as leeches feeding on the bodies of the working people of the world.

They should be banned at once, and the owners and operators be given six months to wind up their operations. From that date forward the law should provide very heavy penalties for anyone designing or operating any system of that sort.

SUMMARY

1.   The Congress of the United States should enact a law authorizing the seizure of the Federal Reserve System without compensation due to its illegitimate birth and the fact that it has been acting in a manner injurious to the American people ever since.

   a.   It is my opinion, and even though I am a Canadian I think I am entitled to have an opinion in this case because not only Americans, but also Canadians and others have suffered injury at the hands of the Fed, any Congressperson or candidate for office who does not aggressively pursue the nationalization of the Fed is a traitor to his or her country and the whole human race.

2.   A newly established Bank of the United States (BUS) should re-establish the policy of cash reserves against deposits at a rate of 5% a year until the reserves have reached a level of 34% which should be the norm going forward.

   a.   The federal government should create non-transferable, non-convertible, non-redeemable shares in the United States to deposit with the BUS as collateral for the cash being provided to the Treasury to be divided 50% federal, 25% state and 25% municipal, debt free.

b. If my old friend Keith Wilde was still alive we could have a nice academic debate as to whether or not the cash is technically debt free. But it is for all practical purposes, and that is all that matters.

c. The advantages as I pointed out earlier include providing governments with sufficient additional cash to balance their books at all levels. No more austerity economics.

d. Equally, if not more important, bank leverages will be reduced to 2 to 1 from 20 to 1 over a seven year period and the banking cartel will have lost its power to run the world!

e. The plan, if applied worldwide will guarantee that there will be no worldwide recession or depression in the wake of the Coronavirus Pandemic. Total world bank deposits are $119,348,976,000.00. Five percent of that figure is $5,967,448,839,500.00. A stimulus of almost $6 trillion—U.S. dollar equivalent— should be adequate to get the world economy up and running on all cylinders.

3. If the United States really wants to be great again it will lead the world in a general disarmament that will pull the planet back from the edge of a nuclear or other disaster. There is evidence that at least once before the human species has been decimated in a nuclear shoot-out, and we must not let it happen again.

a. Cutting defense expenditures by 50% might be enough to thwart the Nazi plan to take over the world, and at the same time lead the world in arresting global warming in seven years and avoiding much of the incalculable devastation that is inevitable with our present trajectory. The world must begin at once to convert from an oil economy to a zero point energy economy (ZPE). Most people have never heard of it, but it is the energy that exists everywhere in the Cosmos, and its free. In the Fourth Edition (2019) of *Zero Point Energy: The Fuel of the Future* Thomas Malone says that Nicola Tesla was the first to describe the real essence of ZPE in 1891.[7] There has been increasing interest over the years with hundreds of experiments and numerous patents.

b. Dr. Michael Wolf (Kruvante), former NSA Consultant in his interview with Chris Stoner, in 2000,[8] said that the United States Armed Forces had developed zero point energy and cold fusion. Of the two I greatly prefer ZPE.

c. It is the third wave of the industrial revolution. First there was the steam engine, powered by coal. Next was the internal combustion engine powered by oil or natural gas. Now there is the third and final zero point energy powered by the inexhaustible energy that exists everywhere in the Universe. It is clean and can be used to rescue the planet!

4. Bitcoins and all cryptocurrencies must be legislated out of existence.

5. A guaranteed annual income must be legislated into existence. It will constitute the biggest social transformation since the abolition of slavery. Certainly more important than the right to vote which all too often does little to provide freedom from hunger, freedom from exploitation and freedom from marginalization. True freedom means being liberated from the shackles of racism and gaining the God given right to be judged by the colour of one's heart, and not the colour of one's skin.

CHAPTER TWELVE

CLEANING UP THE SWAMP

"A person who has ceased learning ought not to be allowed to wander around loose in these dangerous times."

– Anonymous

The Department of Justice is at the top of the list. This decision is based, in part, by what John Loftus has to say in his book *America's Nazi Secret*. It is a story of near total corruption. In addition to the obstruction of justice, the Department has failed to enforce the laws of the United States of America.

Anti-Trust laws may be the most obvious case. The Department of Justice sat idly by as the Bilderbergers, probably the most powerful group in the Cabal that has been running the United States for decades, acquired ownership or editorial control of every major English language news outlet in the U.S., both print and electronic.[1] Consequently the truth about almost every major issue fails to be published while lies, misinformation and disinformation is.

To the best of my knowledge the "shadow government" in control of the U.S. has not told the truth about any major issue from July 8, 1947, when a flying saucer crashed near Roswell, New Mexico. The truth was denied and a substitute story about the discovery having been a Rawin target device, suspended by a Neoprene rubber balloon, was given to the press. That was a lie![2] (Rawin is a method of determining wind speed and direction using radar – sensitive target or radio transponder.)

A case can be made for withholding the truth in 1947, although I strongly prefer transparency. When the Berlin Wall came down, however, and the Soviet Union dissolved, there were no further excuses for hiding the fact that visitors from other realms had visited Earth, and some of them had been working with the U.S. in designing and building a space fleet. Russia and China knew about this, but the U.S. taxpayers and legislators were kept in the dark.

Meanwhile the Justice Department made no serious effort to objectively investigate the dastardly and deadly attack on The World Trade Center in 2001, or to follow all possible leads when reviewing the assassination of a number of prominent Americans who just happened to hold visions for a brighter future that were contrary to those of the Cabal. It is easy to conclude that the FBI had to be complicit in the superficial investigations and conclusions.

I have already recommended that the CIA be wound up immediately and totally. I have provided the reasons why. Such a drastic remedy is impractical in respect of the Department of Justice and the FBI. The future of the Republic may be dependent, however, on a serious purge of the senior echelons in both cases.

It could be based on a new oath, the one that I recommended for all senior officials and military officers beginning with the President of the United States in an earlier book. The rationale was as follows:

The ability of individuals to either directly or indirectly maintain the status quo in the face of essential reforms raises a fundamental and near universal problem. There have been so many of the top jobs filled by nominees recommended by the Cabal for such a long time it would be a miracle if they did not constitute a majority. As stated earlier, no president since Harry Truman could be reasonably assured that his advisors were loyal to the Republic as opposed to the New World Order (NWO). Sorting things out at this stage may be a near impossible task, but some attempt must be made, and without a McCarthy-type witch-hunt.

Perhaps the easiest approach with a reasonable chance of success would be to require everyone on the federal government payroll, including members of the armed forces and intelligence agencies, as well as everyone working for a company with a contract with any branch or agency of the federal government, to swear a supplementary oath to uphold the Constitution of the United States and renounce any allegiance to a New World Order dedicated to a supranational unelected government. I am not competent to draft such an oath; that is a task for experts in the field.

Anyone who is currently supporting the idea of a NWO government of bankers and elite persons who is willing to renounce that allegiance should be allowed to keep their jobs. If, however, by their subsequent actions they show that they have sworn falsely, the prescribed penalty should be ten years in a federal prison. Persons who cannot in conscience swear the oath should be allowed to resign their positions and follow their own "non-sensitive" pursuits.[3]

WIKILEAKS REVEALS US MILITARY USE OF IMF, WORLD BANK AS "UNCONVENTIONAL" WEAPONS

By Whitney Webb, Feb. 7th, 2019.

"In a leaked military manual on 'unconventional warfare' recently highlighted by WikiLeaks, the U.S. Army states that major global financial institutions – such as the World Bank, International Monetary Fund (IMF), and the Organization for Economic Cooperation and Development (OECD) – are used as unconventional, financial 'weapons in times of conflict up to and including large-scale general war,' as well as in leveraging 'the policies and cooperation of state governments.'

"The document, officially titled 'Field Manual (FM) 3-05.130, Army Special Operations Forces Unconventional Warfare' and originally written in September 2008, was recently highlighted by WikiLeaks on Twitter in light of recent events in Venezuela as well as the years-long, U.S.-led economic siege of that country through sanctions and other means of economic warfare. Though the document has generated new interest in recent days, it had originally been released by WikiLeaks in December 2008 and has been described as the military's 'regime change handbook.'

"WikiLeaks' recent tweets on the subject drew attention to a single section of the 248-page-long document, titled 'Financial Instrument of U.S. National Power and Unconventional Warfare.' This section in particular notes that the U.S. government applies 'unilateral and indirect financial power through persuasive influence to international and domestic financial institutions regarding availability and terms of loans, grants, or other financial assistance to foreign state and non-state actors' and specifically names the World Bank, IMF and The Organisation for Economic Co-operation and Development (OECD), as well as the Bank for International Settlements (BIS), as 'U.S. diplomatic-financial venues to accomplish' such goals.

"The manual also touts the 'state manipulation of tax and interest rates' along with other 'legal and bureaucratic measures' to 'open, modify or close financial flows' and further states that the U.S. Treasury's Office of Foreign Assets Control (OFAC) – which oversees U.S. sanctions on other nations, like Venezuela – 'has a long history of conducting economic warfare valuable to any ARSOF [Army Special Operations Forces] UW [Unconventional Warfare] campaign.'

"This section of the manual goes on to note that these financial weapons can be used by the U.S. military to create 'financial incentives or disincentives to persuade adversaries, allies and surrogates to modify their behavior at the theater strategic, operational, and tactical levels' and that such unconventional warfare campaigns are highly coordinated with the State Department and the Intelligence Community in determining 'which elements of the human terrain in UWOA [Unconventional Warfare Operations Area] are most susceptible to financial engagement."[4]

I was already aware of the military aspects of several of these international organizations, but I was surprised and pleased to see it in print from a reputable source. America and the World owe WikiLeaks a debt of gratitude. It may help to understand the extent to which I expressed concern about these institutions in *The Money Mafia: A World In Crisis*.

WIND UP THE IMF

As for the IMF, it should be wound up, and the sooner the better. All the big words used by those who would reform it, words like transparency, enhanced supervision, better monitoring and greater sensitivity, are simply words. You can paint a leopard's spots but that won't change the nature of the beast. Its voracious appetite to interfere cannot be contained, so it must go.

This position has been supported by some very experienced people. Former Secretary of the Treasury, George Shultz, laid out the intellectual case in congressional testimony. He objected to "a pattern of escalation of ambition by the IMF" which would only grow if its request for increased capital was granted. The world financial system would be better off without the IMF, he argued, "because creditors would learn certain lessons. Don't loan money when there are questionable risks. Realize you'll be held accountable for your mistakes."[5]

In his appearance at a hearing of Congress's joint economic committee in May 1998, Shultz repeated and elaborated on arguments he had made earlier in an op-ed piece in the *Wall Street Journal*, which he co-wrote with former Treasury Secretary William Simon and former Citicorp Chairman Walter Wriston. "The IMF is ineffective, unnecessary and obsolete. We do not need another IMF. Once the Asian crisis is over we should abolish the one we have."[6]

A surprising ally was Milton Friedman who endorsed this conclusion in his own op-ed article in the *Wall Street Journal* on October 13, 1998. While not blaming private lenders for accepting the IMF's implicit offer of insurance against currency risk, he did blame the international agency for offering it. Friedman shared my conviction that the U.S. and its allies are derelict in allowing taxpayers' money to be used to subsidize private banks and other financial institutions.

Other critics of the IMF include Harvard economist Jeffrey Sachs and Henry Kissinger, former U.S. Secretary of State in the Nixon era. In an article he wrote for the French newspaper *Le Monde* under the title "The IMF does more harm than good,"

Kissinger said: "It almost always pushes austerity measures that result in a brutal fall in standard of living, an explosive increase in unemployment and poverty." Furthermore, for him, the IMF "is always blind to the consequences of its decisions."[7]

Neither Sachs nor Kissinger recommended abolition of the IMF, settling instead for a modified and considerably reduced role. But that didn't happen. Fast-forward to the 21st century and a stream of financial crises unprecedented since the Great Depression of the 1930s.

An article in the *New York Times* of October 22, 2008, headed "Scandal Hinders IMF's Role in Global Lending," a reference to Dominique Strauss-Kahn, the IMF managing director who was under investigation for alleged impropriety with a former senior official, began as follows:

Washington – "The International Monetary Fund, onetime firefighter for the global economy, is suddenly being called back into action, even as its chief stumbles on his way to the rescue.

"The fund is nearing agreements to make emergency loans to Iceland and Ukraine, and discussing aid packages with Pakistan and Hungary – moves that would thrust it back into the thick of a global crisis after a frustrating period in which it was a bystander.

"It is a welcome return to form for the fund, which lent billions of dollars to crisis-torn economies in Indonesia, Mexico and Argentina – and was later shunned by countries for the strict conditions that it attached to bailouts."[8]

As the size and scope of the European sovereign debt crisis became known it appeared that the IMF would need a large cash infusion to meet the demand. An article in Toronto's *Globe and Mail* on November 3, 2008 reports how the U.K.'s prime minister rode to the rescue.

"A demonstration of how the financial crisis is reordering the world economy was on full display in the Middle East over the weekend. 'First to Kuwait, then Saudi Arabia and then Qatar, British Prime Minister Gordon Brown went cap in hand, asking these emerging market economies for 'hundreds of billions of dollars' to help the International Monetary Fund rescue a growing number of countries from imminent bankruptcy.' 'If we are to stop the spread of the financial crisis, we need a better global insurance policy to help distressed economies,' Mr. Brown, a former U.K. finance minister, told reporters in Riyadh. 'That is why I have called for more resources for the IMF.'"[9]

The problem persisted and became a major item for the G20 world leaders when they met at Cannes, France in November 2011. European leaders were hoping for support in raising the $1.4 trillion bailout fund necessary to prevent countries like Italy and Spain from being part of a larger financial meltdown. But when Canadian Prime Minister Stephen Harper expressed the view that Europe was wealthy enough to solve its own problems, and President Obama concurred, the Europeans were left empty-handed. As the *Toronto Star* reported:

"The best that could be agreed upon was a plan to ask G20 finance ministers to look at measures to add more firepower to the International Monetary Fund, the Washington, D.C.-based institution that acts as the lender of last resort for struggling governments. The finance ministers will take up that task early next year."[10]

The bottom line is that there never will be an acceptable solution to the sovereign debt problem so long as the present insane private banking monopoly remains in place. Bailouts are debt that has to be repaid with interest. But when the IMF is involved the conditions result in more austerity and slower economic growth. Nobel Laureate Joseph Stiglitz, one of the few economists I have heard of who deserves to be read, calls them "beggar-thy-neighbor policies."

"Of all the mistakes the IMF committed as the East Asian crisis spread from one country to another in 1997 and 1998, one of the hardest to fathom was the Fund's failure to recognize the important interactions among the policies pursued in the different countries. Contractionary policies in one country not only depressed that country's economy but had adverse effects on its neighbors. By continuing to advocate contractionary policies the IMF exacerbated the *contagion*, the spread of the downturn from one country to the next. As each country weakened, it reduced its imports from its neighbors, thereby pulling its neighbors down."[11]

Sovereign countries (outside the Eurozone) can print their own money which doesn't have to be paid back. That is a better solution than letting private banks print (computer entry) each country's annual shortfall putting citizens in the hopeless situation of spending the rest of their lives trying to pay it off, with interest.

What the world needs now is not a reformed IMF, even if that were possible; it needs a massive relief from unsustainable debt. Certainly, it does not need an IMF whose principal function is to pass the tin cup for needy banks and financial institutions. The time has come for a clean start without the IMF and without any of the conditions it has imposed on the poorest of the poor. In addition, all of its outstanding loans should be forgiven and written off. For some countries, at least, it would be a small nudge back along the road to prosperity.

A TOBIN TAX

Impose a significant Tobin Tax to provide the relief required for the world's refugees. The Tobin Tax, named after the economist James Tobin, is another idea whose time has come. The idea is to tax every exchange of one country's currency for another. The purpose of the tax is to slow down short-term speculation in currencies. For a number of years about two trillion dollars a day has been involved. The imposition of a small cost - it was originally to be 1% – even a levy of, say, 0.25%, might be enough to make the gamblers pause before making their overnight bets.

While the rationale for a tax of this kind is primarily to create greater stability in financial markets – a worthy cause as we have learned to our total dismay – a secondary benefit would be a steady stream of income that could be earmarked for the U.N. High Commissioner for Refugees (UNHCR) at a time when the need for support has never been greater.

A UNHCR Global Trends report finds 65.3 million people, or one person in 113, were displaced from their homes by conflict and persecution in 2015. The report, entitled "Global Trends," noted that on average, 24 people were forced to flee each minute in 2015, four times more than a decade earlier. It is an unhappy fact that the situation is worse in 2020 than it was then.

A WORLD BANK AND A WORLD DOLLAR

For a number of years there have been increasing tensions between the U.S. and other major powers because the U.S. dollar's role as a global currency has provided that country with a financial advantage. Brazil, Russia, India, and China formed a group that became known as the BRIC group. In 2010 the group added South Africa making its acronym BRICS.

In view of the fact that the existing World Bank, like the IMF, has to be wound up and its debtors forgiven, we can kill two birds with one stone by using the name, World Bank, and its facilities for a new institution.

A solution that would put the U.S. dollar, the euro, the renminbi, the yen and all other currencies on an equal footing, is a new world bank with a new world dollar. It could be called "The Universal," or "Uni," for short. It would be the currency of travelers' checks and of central bank reserves. It would be, in effect, the universal world currency in which all international transactions were denominated.

The new world bank – unlike the Fed or the BIS – must be publicly owned, by the people of the world, under a formula that would prevent undue influence from any country or region. Its assets would comprise very large deposits of all world currencies and gold. Each would be convertible into any other at market prices, as the bank would be the *de facto* bank of international settlements, replacing the highly secretive existing Bank for International Settlements (BIS), with its shadowy past and Nazi connections, that is an accessory to the system that had been running the world into the ground.

There is considerable urgency in this area. The Chinese are dissatisfied with the long-standing American monopoly and the early establishment of a universally backed world currency, would forestall a lot of jockeying for position. It would effectively end the diplomatic, financial and sometimes shooting wars over possession of the endless supply of golden eggs.

ROLL THE WORLD TRADE ORGANIZATION BACK TO A GENERAL AGREEMENT ON TRADE AND TARIFFS

The World Trade Organization itself was not intended to help the poor. It was designed to enhance and consolidate the power of the elite at the expense of the poor nations and poor people. It, too, has transferred far too much sovereignty from nation states to unelected, unaccountable bureaucrats working under rules actually written by, or at the behest of, the chief executive officers of multinational corporations.

The concept of a rules-based system is great in theory. It sounds very reasonable. But surely not just one set of rules applying to all countries equally?

The World Boxing Federation has fifteen classes including flyweight, lightweight, middleweight and heavyweight. I would guess that the world's many different countries could be classified in as many as fifteen different categories. *Certainly not just one!* The WTO rules were written by, or on behalf of, the heavyweights for the benefit of heavyweights. The result is a trade regime under which everyone else is going to be clobbered.

The second objection is, as I said, the loss of democracy. The WTO exercises de facto executive, judicial and legislative powers equivalent to that of a world government. These powers were transferred to it without the advice or consent of the peoples affected. Apologists for the WTO say that consent was granted when people elected the governments which did the deal. But that is a cop-out. The governments neither told their electors what was involved, nor asked their opinion about it. Needless to say this was deliberate policy on the part of governments attempting to serve two masters.

The only satisfactory remedy is to abolish the WTO and go back to the General Agreement on Tariffs and Trade (GATT) from which it sprang. From there we can build a trade regime which preserves the essential powers of nation states, recognizes the different needs of countries based on size, population and state of development, and provides the flexibility for cooperative rather than coercive relationships. For want of a better description, I call them the "Marquess of Queensberry" Rules of Trade.

THE MARQUESS OF QUEENSBERRY RULES FOR TRADE AND INVESTMENT

- Fair trade, not "free trade." There is no such thing as genuine free trade, as Canada has found in its relationship with the U.S.

- Every country should have the right to protect some of its infant industries. If it doesn't, they will never grow to adulthood.

- Every country has the right to determine the conditions under which direct foreign investment is welcome.

- Every country has the right to impose controls on the movement of short-term capital in cases of emergency.

- Every country has the right to determine the limits of foreign ownership in each area of economic activity.

- Every nation state should have the right to decide what trade concessions it will put on the table in exchange for others as was the case under the GATT.

- Every country should have control over its own banking system.

- Every country has the right to use and should use its own central bank to assist in the financing of essential services and to keep the economy operating at or near its potential at all times.

- Rich countries should be encouraged to license the use of their technology by poor countries at modest cost.

- Every country should be obligated to cooperate with other countries in the protection of the oceans, their species, the ozone layer and in all ways essential to protect the Earth's ecosystem for the benefit of future generations.

- Every country should be encouraged to maintain some control of its own food supply, to the extent practical, and not become dependent on patented seeds and products.

- Every country should be encouraged to pass a law amending corporate charters in a way that would require directors to consider the interests of all stakeholders, and not just those of shareholders when making decisions.

- Every country should have the right, and should be encouraged, to develop and maintain a significant degree of self-sufficiency in the production of goods and services for the use and enjoyment of its own people. The objective should be to reduce its vulnerability to the vagaries of decisions made by others and the unexpected such as the Coronavirus Pandemic of 2020.[12]

Some may say that I am proposing a return to a "protectionist" world. Let me put it another way. I am proposing a system where the rights and interests of billions of people are protected from the predators – so the rich barons do not have unrestricted license to poach on other people's estates.

The New World Order is a gigantic hoax. It is not interested in trade. Its plan is centralized ownership and control as a means to facilitate a world government under its control. Its brand of globalization is a greed-driven monster legitimized by academic abstractions far removed from the real world and real people.

Fundamentalist economics is a numbers game, in which people are digits. They are counted, sorted, exploited when useful, and abandoned when surplus. It would be numerically inefficient to treat them otherwise. The system I am proposing is one where human beings are entitled to a status greater than inanimate objects - one where they will have some control over their own lives and destiny. Such a system would be closer to the model of nature, where babies and children are protected until they reach maturity and can compete on their own. Even then, there are physical and intellectual differences between adults that must be taken into account.

What I am proposing is the transformation of a system that is immoral and inefficient, into one that is fundamentally moral and much more efficient - a system where everyone, everywhere, can hope for better things to come.

MASSIVELY REDUCE DEFENSE EXPENDITURES AND ATOMIC WEAPONS WORLDWIDE

While the United States can afford to reduce defense expenditures by 50% unilaterally without compromising its security, it is only fair in a world that can only survive by shifting to a new paradigm, that all countries shift their priorities from defense and war-making capability to peace and international cooperation. A combination of a positive banking system, and major reductions in arms expenditures, will provide each country with the financial flexibility necessary to subsidize the transformation to clean energy, with enough left over to increase expenditures on a wide range of initiatives to improve the quality of life for its citizens.

Then there is the question of reducing nuclear stockpiles. In a sane world none of these weapons can be used under any circumstances! Ever! The risk for the planet is too great and the extraterrestrial consequences too alarming. So it is ridiculous for the U.S. to still have missiles on alert in silos in the Midwest. All it can possibly justify is a few submarine missile carriers – just enough to guarantee the "mutually assured destruction (MAD)" that should deter even a madman from launching an attack.

Consequently I fully support a recommendation of the 2006 Weapons of Mass Destruction Commission, i.e. number 19 under "Nuclear Weapons."

"Russia and the United States, followed by other states possessing nuclear weapons, should publish their aggregate holdings of nuclear weapons on active and reserve status as a baseline for future disarmament efforts. They should also agree to include specific provisions in future disarmament agreements relating to transparency, irreversibility, verification and the physical destruction of nuclear warheads."[13]

That is a very modest beginning. It should be followed by an immediate reduction of stockpiles to the absolute minimum consistent with mutually assured deterrence and as a protection against cheating.

Any nation refusing to cooperate should be subject to severe sanctions like a 10% tariff on all its exports to be increased each year of non-compliance. The existence of atomic weapons is a threat to the viability of the planet itself, and any person or nation that even contemplates circumstances under which they might be used should be the subject of universal condemnation.

A similar but greatly accelerated plan should apply to biological and chemical weapons.

A LIMIT ON EXECUTIVE SALARIES

In the early '90s CEO salaries were about forty times the average salary of their employees. Since then they have escalated to 237 times (one report says 433) on average – ratios that cannot be justified by any economic or moral standard, and still rising!

Inevitably it will be argued that big bonuses are warranted as a reward for extraordinary corporate results. It is an argument for which there is a counter argument. Doing a good job is what CEOs are paid for, and their principal satisfaction should be in a job well done. Rewarding short-term results has often resulted in short-term planning at the expense of a longer-term vision. Equally perverse, the culture of exorbitant rewards has become so all pervasive that it extends even to mediocre results and separation agreements.

This example of greed and avarice is totally unacceptable. How can you ask union leaders to accept increases of 2% or less, let alone reductions in pay to make companies more competitive, when executives are given double or triple digit increases?

Executive compensation including salary, bonuses, stock options and retirement benefits should be limited to fifty times the average for their employees and any excess should be subject to a 100% excess profit tax, in order to end the abuse of privilege.

VACCINES

I have a number of friends who are against Vaccines. Period. I am not one of them because I remember how vaccines have been used to control, and in some cases eliminate many serious diseases. In particular, I remember the fear of polio (poliomyelitis) when I was young. Thanks to Dr. Jonas Salk it has been removed from the list of concerns.

At the same time I share the increasing concern about the abuse of vaccines. Robert Kennedy Jr. has sounded an alarm bell that everyone should hear. So I am repeating it here:

"A 2017 study (Morgensen et. Al. 2017) showed that WHO's popular Diphtheria, Tetanus and Pertussis (DTP) vaccine is killing more African children than the diseases it pretends to prevent. Vaccinated girls suffered 10x the death rate of unvaccinated children. The extremely wealthy Bill Gates and the world health organization (WHO) have refused to recall the lethal vaccine which WHO forces upon millions of African children annually.

"Global public health advocates around the world accuse Gates of hijacking WHO's agenda away from the projects that are proven to curb infectious diseases; clean water, hygiene, nutrition, and economic development. They say he has diverted agency resources to serve his personal fetish – that good health only comes in a syringe.

"In addition to using his philanthropy to control WHO, UNICEF, GAVI, and PATH, Gates funds private pharmaceutical companies that manufacture vaccines, and a massive network of pharmaceutical-industry front groups that broadcast deceptive propaganda, develop fraudulent studies, conduct surveillance and psychological operations against vaccine hesitancy and use Gates' power and money to silence dissent and coerce compliance. In his recent non-stop Pharmedia appearances, Gates appears gleeful that the COVID-19 crisis will give him the opportunity to force his third-world vaccine programs on American children.

"During Gates' 2002 MenAfruVac campaign in Sub-Saharan Africa, Gates' operatives forcibly vaccinated thousands of African children against meningitis. Between 50 and 500 children developed paralysis. South African newspapers complained, 'We are guinea pigs for the drug makers.' Nelson Mandela's former Senior Economist, Professor Patrick Bond, describes Gates' philanthropic practices as 'ruthless and immoral.'

"In 2010, Gates committed $10 billion to the WHO promising to reduce population, in part, through new vaccines. A month later, Gates told a Ted Talk that new vaccines 'could reduce population.' In 2014, Kenya's Catholic Doctors' Association accused the WHO of chemically sterilizing millions of unwilling Kenyan women with a phony 'tetanus' vaccine campaign. Independent labs found the sterility formula in every vaccine tested. After denying the charges, WHO finally admitted it had been developing the sterility vaccines for over a decade. Similar accusations came from Tanzania, Nicaragua, Mexico, and the Phillipines."[14]

I Paul, hereby attest that I will not agree to be vaccinated with any Coronavirus vaccine until I know where it was developed, and by whom, including the sponsorship and knowledge of who is paying for it.

BANKING PRACTICES AND REGULATIONS

Taming the international banking system will be a monumental challenge but it simply has to be done. The items will be in brief because I have already recorded how amoral the system is, and there is no need to repeat it.

The first is a change in the law to take away their right to either own stocks and bonds, or to trade in them. They are bankers not brokers and they shouldn't be in the business because they have enough money power to rig the market. The wealthy elite win and everyone else loses.

Next is the question of derivatives. Never has so much energy and intellectual ingenuity been used for the benefit of the giants in the ring. They should be granted a reasonable length of time to get them off their books and be prohibited from getting them back on again.

The third big one is the practice of short selling. I have a friend named Danny who has been keeping me informed on this iniquitous practice. In one extreme case more shares had been shorted than the total capitalization of the company. It is a complicated subject but I recently reviewed a copy of an article entitled *"License to Steal, STOP THE NAKED SHORT SELLING OF AMERICA."*

It is an open letter to President Donald Trump by Larry Smith dated May 26, 2020. I am sorry that I can't include the visuals of a pack of voracious wolves sitting around a table bearing a large roasted pig labelled "TARGETED COMPANY" with its identification "FEAST OF THE NAKED SHORTS." Here is the letter, in part.

"Mr. President,

"Mr. Robert David Steele and I were recently introduced by mutual acquaintances. All of us share one major conviction. We believe that hedge funds working in collusion with certain elite Wall Street investment banks are engaged in a long running, unbelievably broad, criminal enterprise to manipulate stocks. (I have labeled the participants as the wolfpack.) This scam defrauds investors of hundreds (yes hundreds) of billions of dollars each year and causes incalculable damage to companies, particularly the emerging companies that are the most vulnerable to their stock manipulation. Integral to their strategy is the use of illegal naked shorting to create and sell huge amounts of counterfeit stock to depress stock prices. This is a crime against society as it is these entrepreneurial companies that most often lead technological evidences that drive the American economy.

"The wolfpack is driven by insatiable greed. It is not enough to have a home in Greenwich, a summer home in the Hamptons, a condo in Miami, an apartment in New York City, a ski chalet in Aspen, private planes, cars, ad infinitum. They just want to make their next billion dollars and if it means destroying a small company trying to develop a vaccine for brain cancers, this is just business as usual. Most recently, I have watched with consternation attacks on Gilead, which is developing a therapeutic for COVID-19 (remdesivir), and Moderna which is developing a vaccine for COVID-19. The wolfpack was successful in driving down the stock prices of Gilead and Moderna as well as the market as a whole using bloggers to spread negative fake news and then pounding the stocks with shorts. These were nice scores for the wolfpack. This sounds like wild hyperbole, but sadly I do not believe that I am overstating the case and if you decide to look further, I think you will agree."[15]

I have looked further, and I am prepared to roundly condemn the practice of short-selling because it is basically a crime to buy and sell something that you don't own. I have heard all the stories about the benefit of short-selling to put pressure on incompetent management. There are honest ways of dealing with that problem. Short-selling is not one of them. It should be a criminal offence!

THE PALESTINIAN-ISRAELI SWAMP

This is one of the biggest and most enduring swamps of all. Numerous attempts have been made to reach an agreement between the two parties but always without success, for the simple reason that the Israelis didn't want one. They went through the process to satisfy world opinion, but never with the intent of reaching a fair deal for both parties.

Chapter 10 that you have just read puts a whole new light on the situation. The Khazarian Israelis used a combination of brute force and very large amounts of money to gain a foothold in Palestine, and then gain United Nations support for national status comprising the lion's share of the Palestinian land.

I have just re-read "AN OFFICIAL UN REPORT A SUMMARY OF THE ZIONIST TERRORISM IN THE NEAR EAST – 1944 – 1948, PREPARED BY DR. RALPH J. BUNCHE, UN MEDIATOR FOR PALESTINE." I must say that it sounds a lot more like the Khazarian Mafia than it does the sons of Abraham. The dots are beginning to connect.

In effect the Khazarian Jews were not entitled to any of the promised land of Palestine because they were not descendants of Abraham, and not beneficiaries of his promise.

This verdict is reinforced by the fact that some of the Khazarian bankers had helped finance Hitler's Nazis when they were torturing and killing thousands of Abrahamic Jews. It is the Palestinians who are the Semites, the sons and daughters of Abraham and Ishmael, who are the rightful heirs of about 80 percent of Palestine. So the Khazarians encroachment on the West Bank, and Netanyahu's threat to annex that land is absolutely null and void!

The world community, hopefully with United Nations approval, must order the Israelis to withdraw to their original borders. All of the stolen or purchased Palestinian land must be given up and the buildings left in perfect condition as partial restitution for the years of harassment and worse. Even the smallest change in the border would have to be one negotiated by mutual agreement. In addition, the Israelis should be required to build a dedicated transportation corridor to connect the Gaza strip with the West Bank so there can be a greater unity in a New Palestinian State.

There would be benefits all around. The Arab League was willing, and should still be willing to accept Israel as a State, so peace and cooperation should prevail on all sides. At last, with U.S. cooperation in removing troops from sacred Islamic ground, the terms of peace, set out by the late Osama Bin Laden, would be achieved. The following was his advice to U.S. President George W. Bush.

> "Every Muslim must rise to defend his religion. The wind of faith is blowing and the wind of change is blowing to remove evil from the Peninsula of Muhammad, peace be upon him. As to America, I say to it and its people a few words: I swear to God that Americans will not live in peace before peace reigns in Palestine, and before the army of infidels depart the land of Muhammad, peace be upon him."[15]

In the event the Khazarian Israelis are reluctant to support the fair settlement and peace plan, they should be subject to worldwide sanctions, similar to the ones imposed on Iran by the U.S., possibly at Israeli request. The price of worldwide acceptance of the Khazarian Israelis has to be full acceptance of a Palestinian state with the right of return to that state but not to Israel. This kind of reconciliation based on cooperation would constitute a giant step toward peace in the Middle East.

The Israelis must know that they have lost their special status with the God of Abraham, Isaac, Jacob and Ishmael. There are a number of reasons, including:

1. You have treated the Palestinians abominably.

2. You covet someone else's land.

3. You don't observe the Golden Rule.

4. Some of your leaders worship Baal aka Lucifer, Satan, the Evil one.

5. The dastardly and deadly attack on the World Trade Center in New York, September 11, 2001.

6. Your Prime Minister, Benjamin Netanyahu has been providing a secret German Nazi group with atomic weapons in exchange for submarines capable of firing missiles like the one that hit the Pentagon in Washington D.C., Sept 11, 2001.

Consequently you have lost the right to call Jerusalem your own. The Holy City must be internationalized and governed by a council of not less than six and not more than twelve persons with equal representation from each of the Abrahamic Religions, Christianity, Islam and Judaism. It must become a beacon of inclusivity.

OBJECTIVITY

It is almost inevitable that I will be accused of being anti-Semitic. That would not be true.

From my earliest days on the farm there was a close connection with the Jewish people. Hellyer Brothers, my father and uncle Russell, sold all of their ginseng to Jewish fur brokers in New York. Then, as a teenager, when I was old enough to trap muskrats, I sold all of my fur pelts to the same firm.

When I was discharged from the military in 1946, and moved to Toronto with my late wife Ellen and our baby daughter, we had to buy a business with an apartment above in order to get a place to live because there were no places for rent anywhere in the city. We finally settled on a Ladies Ready-To-Wear Store on Bloor St. near Dufferin. Rae Anger, a short dark Jewish lady, was our senior saleslady for eleven years until the building was sold. We became so close that Rae had nightmares about who she would save first if her grand-daughter and our daughter were both drowning. Our suppliers of dresses, suits and coats, were all Jewish and we established close working relationships.

Then, years later, I ran for the leadership of the Liberal Party of Canada in 1958, my Toronto campaign manager was Major (Ret.) Barney Danson, one of the nicest human beings that I have ever known. We recruited the support of every senior Jewish Liberal in the city with the exception of one, Senator David Croll, who had good reason for withholding his support. I became the first Liberal Member of Parliament from Toronto to be appointed to a federal cabinet in history when Dave, and many others of us, thought the honor should have been his. We remained friends, but his supporters would not have understood if he had supported me at the Liberal Convention.

These are just a few of the highlights of my relationship with the Jewish community. My friends were descendants of Abraham, and almost invariably they were nice and a joy to know The moral of the story is that I seek the truth in all circumstances, and proclaim it without fear or favor.

CHAPTER THIRTEEN

LET THE LIGHT SHINE IN

"Seek ye the truth for the truth will set you free."
– John 8:32

The world is in one gosh awful mess and our future as a species depends on what we do about it. Fifty years ago it was popular to say that education was the solution to our problems. Looking back in 2020 we know that some of the best educated and greatest minds have been dedicated to the development of newer and more efficient ways of killing people. It is true that better and more affordable access to educational facilities would be beneficial to millions of the world's poorest children, but it wouldn't guarantee them access to useful employment.

I have also heard it said that what we need is more of that old fashion religion. Really? In a book titled *Light at the End of the Tunnel: A Survival Plan for the Human Species,* I quote from a Top Secret letter from Canada's ambassador to the Soviet Union, Robert A.D. Ford, who blamed religion as a principal cause of strife and conflict in the world. I thought of myself as a "religious" person, so I took some offense.

As the years went by I came to realize that Ambassador Ford had a more mature worldview than I did. Some of my subsequent studies included major wars and atrocities that history recorded as being of religious origin. These were in the past tense but I soon realized they had never stopped. It is as much a part of the late twentieth and early twenty-first centuries as it was of earlier times. All over the world people are still fighting and dying in support of their religious beliefs.

I wrote several pages of old and recent examples of religious conflicts between Buddhists and Hindus, Communists and Buddhists, Hindus against Muslims, Sikhs against Hindus and other examples to illustrate the point. A reader pointed out to me that in some of those examples there were other factors than religion such as tribalism and territorialism. Consequently, I reduced the number of stories to a mere handful sufficient to underline the continuing nature of these complicated conflicts, and the absolute necessity of finding means of resolving them without resorting to the use of force.

The list included Christians Against Muslims, Christians Against Christians, Christians Against Jews, Jews Against Muslim and Christian Palestinians, Muslims Against Christians, Muslims Against Jews, and Muslims Against Muslims. Each story is interesting, and reminds us of just how fragile human relations really are, and the importance of addressing some of the fundamental issues. Each religion claims that one of its cardinal beliefs is some form of the Golden Rule, treating a brother or sister, as you would wish to be treated if the roles were reversed. In reality, not one of the religions practices it.

DIALOGUE IS THE FIRST STEP

The day I began to write this chapter I was leafing through the *New York Times International Weekly June 12-14, 2020,* to be greeted by Father's Beheading of Girl Horrifies Iranians. I am sure it did, it certainly horrified me. A box in the article read **"An honor killing puts a new focus on women's rights."** I should hope so.

The dreadful war in Yemen, and the years-long civil war in Syria, that has killed thousands and dislocated millions of innocent families and their children, are two more horror stories. A third would be the Islamic State, a group that has been indoctrinated with the "superiority complex syndrome," the root of many of the world's past and current evils.

For several years now I have been recommending dialogue. Miracles can happen, witness the remarkable reconciliation between Catholics and Protestants in the Christian faith. That is a good news story. The continuing conflict between Shias and Sunni Muslims is a blot on the history of Islam. The problem is deeply rooted in power and politics even though both worship the same God, and revere the same holy book, the Qu'ran. It is shameful that both the U.S. and Russia pick sides and provide armaments to nations or factions without which the various conflicts would be more difficult, if not impossible, to continue.

The UN needs to initiate two open-ended conferences. The first should include all of the major religions sitting down at the same table and getting to know each other. They can look for commonality of purpose. They can also look for out-dated anomalies such as honor killing and death for apostasy. The Israelites have adapted many of their ancient practices to reflect a more modern view of the Creator's wishes, and the Muslims and Christians should look at some of their rules and regulations with equally open hearts and minds.

The second conference should be for Sunnis and Shias only. They simply must end their age-old conflict and effect a reconciliation that would allow them to work hand-in-hand to help build God's kingdom here on Earth. I would suggest that former U.S. Congressman Mark Siljander, who has learned Arabic in order to build bridges between Christians and Islam, act as a neutral chair. He has told me that he could recruit one moderate Shia Imam and one moderate Sunni Imam to assist him in one of the greatest, most important challenges of our time.[1]

Mark is also an expert in the doctrinal gap between Christianity and Islam. In his marvellously insightful book *A Deadly Misunderstanding: A Congressman's Quest to Bridge the Muslim-Christian Divide,* he describes the narrow gulf between Christian factions that separate us from our Muslim brothers and sisters.

"At one point the raging debate between Christians boiled down to a disagreement between two words – actually, to be more precise, between *two letters* in a word. One group wanted to describe Jesus as *homoiousious,* 'of a *similar* substance' to God, while another insisted that he be described as *homoousious,* 'of the *same* substance' as God. Constantine came down on the side of the homoousians, and thus today we have the Nicene Creed, which declares that Jesus is 'begotten, not made, being *of one substance* with the Father.'" I will re-open this debate later in the chapter.

EUROPEAN CHRISTIANS OF CONVENIENCE

A time came when a number of European countries including Spain, Holland, Belgium, France and England set out to conquer the world. It was a classic case of "superiority complex." Africans, South and North Americans, and some Asians were the principal targets. Their peoples were invariably considered as inferior in intellect and culture, so the Europeans considered it fair game to conquer and use them and their resources to their own advantage. Tragically, the European superiority was largely based on the possession of more and bigger guns.

When the French and English began to colonize North America the assumption was that the Natives, because they didn't have European technology, were some kind of inferior beings. That old "superiority complex" ruled the day. Consequently, they were exploited and driven from their ancestral territories.

There appeared to be little if any change in attitude when the British conquered the French province of Quebec, as a first step toward the bilingual federation called Canada. Sir John A. Macdonald was the man most responsible for creating the country we now know as Canada. His attitude toward the Aboriginals was typical: "You can educate them all you want, and they will still be savages." He was wrong! Wrong! Wrong!

When people of the First Nations are provided with equal educational and other opportunities they are as good and as useful as any of us. In some ways they are superior. They have a greater respect for Gaia, our living breathing planet, and treat it with the reverence it deserves. In an earlier chapter I pointed out that when it came to a choice between saving the planet by abandoning the oil economy before it is too late, it was three Hereditary Chiefs who took the long view on behalf of our grandchildren and great-grandchildren. There are substitutes for jobs in the oil and gas industry, but there is no convenient alternative to a habitable planet.

The Canadian federation is not an easy country to govern. The English speakers, as the majority were known, when I was first elected in 1949, assumed that in some way we were superior to the French speakers. Parliament operated almost exclusively in English, from the elevator operators, to the top jobs. With the exception of External Affairs, nearly all of the senior cabinet positions including Finance, Industry, Defence and Transport were held by English speakers.

Most of us were not fluently bilingual, so each department would have an assistant deputy minister from Quebec who could translate for us when receiving delegations from that province. Eventually, the tide began to turn. We adopted simultaneous translation in the House of Commons. When Pierre Elliot Trudeau became prime minister he began appointing French speakers to important portfolios. Today French speakers have equality or better and they have proven that their performance is as good as anybody else.

One final paragraph on this subject. In the province of Quebec that is predominantly French speaking, the English speakers ran most of the industry and exercised the prerogatives of the conqueror. Jean LeSage, who had been a federal cabinet minister, moved to Quebec politics as Premier and presided over what became known as the Silent revolution that eventually gave Quebec as much or more autonomy as they would have had under the European Mastrich Treaty, that had been the separatist leader's goal.

French is the predominant language and native Quebecois are in complete control. The moral of the story is that the province is run at least as well as the other Canadian provinces and, on some occasions, they have been leaders in important reforms. The "superiority complex" of the English speakers was just a myth.

MINORITIES ALWAYS GET THE SHORT END OF THE STICK

The above is a good news story for the French speakers in Quebec, but hasn't guaranteed their rights in other provinces. The same problems have developed regarding English speakers who live in Quebec. But there are other minorities who suffer more. They include the Aboriginals, Blacks, Asians, Muslims, Jews, the handicapped, the LGBTQ communities, and recent immigrants before they get established. They all have to row upstream.

Some progress is being made. The LGBTQ Community in Canada has made great strides in the last decade or so. The church I attend is an Affirming Church, where all are welcome. The recent decision of the Supreme Court of the United States to the effect that individuals can no longer lose their jobs due to their sexual orientation is a giant step forward. But there are still some very sad cases.

WHAT GOD HAS CREATED LET NO MAN DISDAIN

The Bible is my favourite book. I have read it from cover to cover three times. I always take it seriously, but not always literally. A classic case relates to homosexuality where a literal reading has caused great injustice, injury, pain and heartache. I would go so far as to say that it is not homosexuality that is the abomination; that word more appropriately applies to the consequences of treating passages like Romans Chapter 1 vs 26-27 as a divine proclamation. The Holy Spirit undoubtedly influenced the content of the Bible but a careful reading suggests that too often the Spirit was trumped by the prejudiced views of macho men. You certainly did not hear any condemnation of homosexuality coming from the mouth of Jesus when he was on Earth.

Full acceptance really requires getting to know homosexuals as individuals and this can be a lifelong learning process. One of the young men in the Bible class I taught was gay. He and his partner entered into a lifelong relationship. He has played an active role in a successor Bible class and took his turn as president with full support of the membership.

One of my grandsons is gay, and the characteristics were clear from the time he was a young child. It only became official when Joshua turned twenty-one and wrote a delightful little autobiography titled *Give Life a Squeeze: Juicy Observations from my Life's First Quarter*, disclosing his personal journey of acceptance in the hope it might help other young people who struggle with their sexuality. He is wonderfully supported by all the members of the family who love him dearly and unreservedly.

Not all homosexuals are as fortunate. Two case studies from real life are illustrative. The Calgary, Alberta, Prayer Breakfast Group membership was primarily but not exclusively comprised of urban businessmen whose theology and politics were both decidedly conservative. They assumed that their waiter was gay and whispered slurs loudly enough for him to hear.

Outraged by the insult he asked to be heard. He told the group that he was a born again Christian who had a Masters degree in theology. His father, the senior pastor at a conservative evangelical church in the United States, had completely disowned him years earlier, and refused to see either him or his partner. He reminded the group that Christianity is supposed to be an inclusive religion that celebrates the value and dignity of all people. Nevertheless the group decided to change their meeting place much to the dismay of the female members, and one or two of the more liberal participants.

I was witness to a good news story on the same subject. One Wednesday morning, just before Christmas, one of the more conservative members of the Prayer Breakfast Group that I attend shared that his daughter had just told him that she was gay. His first instinct, he told us, was to ask her to move out and never darken his doorstep again.

To a man, every one of us advised him to go home, put his arms around his daughter and tell her he loved her and wanted her to be home for Christmas. Furthermore her partner would be welcome, too. And that is what he did.

The litmus test of our sincerity is the Golden Rule. If, by accident of birth, we were "one of them" would we want to be subject to stinging slurs and epithets? Or would we want to be fully accepted as one of God's glorious variety of children and allowed to joyfully share our common heritage?

FREEDOM FOR THE SLAVES

We learned when researching the Khazarians that they may have been involved in the slavetrade. That doesn't absolve the British and American Christians, and to a smaller extent Canadians, from one of the most despicable practices imaginable. The circumstances of their transport across the ocean is almost horrible beyond description. And what could be more humiliating than to be sold at auction. Some were treated better than others, but they were slaves nevertheless, with the same legal status as cattle.

The hard-headedness of the "superiority complex cohort," as the debate about freeing the slaves began, was very disturbing. William Wilberforce, a member of the British parliament and some of his friends were key players, but it was a long and uphill battle. In the United States it required a civil war. On January 1, 1863, President Lincoln formally issued the Emancipation Proclamation, calling on the Union Army to liberate all slaves in states still in rebellion as "an act of justice, warranted by the Constitution, upon military necessity."[2]

The approximately 3.9 million slaves were all ultimately freed, but had freedom to do what? They could shine shoes, tend railway sleeping cars, pick crops, clean houses and work as cooks if, in fact, they could get a job. Eventually there were a few exceptions for a few excellent football and basketball players whose lights shone like Roman candles in the night. There was no genuine equality of opportunity either in the U.S. or Canada.

It is true, however, that not even the stars in the world of sport, or the occasional black lawyer or doctor, was immune from harassment from the police. If one of them happened to have a better than average car the odds were they would be pulled over and asked to prove that they were the rightful owner. The police have demonstrated systemic racism and enhanced physicality toward blacks for as long as I can remember.

There have been occasional stories of police shootings, but those are the kind of stories that keep newspapers in business. They are routine, and don't attract much attention. Then, one evening, the TV news reported that George Floyd, a black man had been brutally murdered by the Minneapolis police. The whole gruesome scene was flashed before our eyes. It was worse than war. How could any human being so calmly snuff out the life of another human being?

When the Avaaz Group sent an email listing word for word and second by second Mr. Floyd's pleas to let him live, I was affected as I have never been affected before. I knew instinctively that this was going to be a watershed in history. Protest demonstrations seemed to appear by magic. Riots followed as decades of oppression and marginalization broke through the dam of restraint.

Almost as if on cue the demonstrations spread across the United States, Canada, Europe and the Far East. The days of discontent continued and the protestors of principle were joined by Aboriginals, the handicapped, new immigrants and others all proclaiming that Black Lives Matter. Aboriginal lives matter, handicapped lives matter, Muslim lives matter, Jewish lives matter. The message was loud and clear. No one can claim superiority. We are all literally God's children formed from particles from the Creator's body, and we should treat each other as brothers and sisters. We are in fact siblings!

I am not going to enter the realm of police budgets, but I do think the police need to be deprogrammed to remove some of the militarism that forms part of their training, and take some courses on ethics and how to live by the Golden Rule. They are hired to serve and protect us but they should be taught to think of the Golden Rule. If they were the one being arrested would they want to be unnecessarily subject to a chokehold? And if they tried to run away would they like to be shot in the back when they provided no immediate threat to anyone?

The bottom line, unfortunately, is that we are all racists. I have met people who said they were not racist, but if you scratch beneath the surface for a while you will find that they are not without prejudice. It is something we have to accept, and fight against for our whole lives. We should remember that we are, literally, all children of the same Creator God and, as siblings, we should make a special effort to remember when we see someone who is handicapped, or of a different color, **that we are equally loved and treasured.**

BIBLICAL ALLEGORIES

A couple of weeks ago the scripture reading at our church was the first chapter of the book of Genesis.[3] The story is about God creating the Heavens and the Earth in six days. Regretfully, there was no caveat to inform listeners that this was just a story. It is not history.[4] Still I have met mature (in age) Christians who are absolutely convinced that the world was created in six twenty-four-hour days. This kind of naivety makes me sad.

The same is true with the creation of man and woman. Life on Earth did not begin with Adam and Eve in the Garden of Eden. That was just a few thousand years ago according to the Biblical story. Yet ancient humans lived in China 2.1 million years ago.[5]

All of the things described in the first two chapters of Genesis actually happened. But instead of being accomplished in six 24-hour days, it took thousands of millions of years.[6]

It is of little consequence for us to know if, or when, the story of the Genesis account of Adam and Eve happened because we can learn from this story. The primary lesson from the story is the nature of the temptation. The enemy of God told Adam and Eve that if they disobeyed and ate the fruit from the tree of knowledge they would not die. They would be like God. At the heart of all the evil documented in this book and all the evil happening in the world are people who are driven to be gods. They want to be in charge –to control others for their own self-centered ends.

In my view the reality of creation does not pit the creationists against the evolutionists. They are just two different perceptions of reality. God did create everything that exists beginning with the big bang more than 13 billion years ago by setting the rules as to how the trillions of particles would coalesce and form the gorgeous cosmos we are part of. (See the NASA sketch of the time line from the Big Bang until now, in the picture section at the back of the book.) [7]

The reality also settles the dispute Mark Siljander found. Jesus was not God as he himself pointed out so clearly. He is a Son of God in the literal sense, as we are all sons and daughters of the Creator. Jesus was and is a highly-evolved favored son who agreed to come to Earth in human form to show us the real face of God as one of love and compassion. This was to offset the Old Testament false picture that portrayed God as a ruthless warmonger, counselling the massacre of men, women and children before stealing their land. These were the practices recommended by the Elohim, a highly-advanced group from another planet or star system who, when they arrived on Earth in their space vehicles, were perceived as gods and received as such. Jesus set the record straight! God loves all of his/her children and it doesn't matter about the color of their skin or their sexual orientation. God does not play favorites. (For a more extensive discussion on the Creation of the Cosmos read chapter 23, *"God is Alive, Well, and Everywhere"* in *Hope Restored, An Autobiography.*

Coming back to Earth, we have gotten ourselves into a terrible mess by not observing either of the two great commandments of the Creator as given to Moses and repeated by Jesus. The first is **"Thou shalt love the Lord thy God with all thy heart and soul and strength and mind,"** and the second is **"Thou shalt love thy neighbour as thyself."** The most powerful people in the World hate God and worship Ba'al, aka The Devil, Satan, Lucifer or the Evil One. Lucifer, too, is a highly-evolved Son of God, but one who decided he should be king. So he has been recruiting adversaries of the Lord in the hope that he can establish a kingdom of power and strength.

His allies on Earth include the Khazarian Illuminati and the Nazi party, as well as an alien species known as the Reptilians, or Reptoids. Len Kasten, one of the best-informed ufologists, has written that the Reptilians have been living underground on Earth. From their subterranean bases they have been supporting the German Nazis from long before World War II and ever since as they plan to play god, establish the Fourth Reich and exterminate most of the rest of us. They are the joint sponsors of all five plagues that I mentioned at the outset.

NOW THE GOOD NEWS

I have ended my last two books with a few examples of the wonderful things that are happening all over the world. Inspired individuals are creating small miracles of hope and love in action. I will not repeat them all here, with two exceptions.

Not all of the good news stories claim religious connection. Avaaz, a global web movement, sponsors many important initiatives. Danny, Alice, Alison, Marigona, Ricken, Iain and the rest of their team are world leaders in drawing attention to injustices, industrial excess and world problems of all kinds. One of their appeals really got my attention.

> Dear Friends,
>
> "15,000 scientists just sent out an SOS – a "warning to humanity" that if we don't stop polluting, our planet is doomed.
>
> "The facts are terrifying: species are going extinct at 1,000 times the natural rate. 90% of the Great Barrier Reef is dead or dying. Oceans are so choked with plastic that fish are addicted to eating it.
>
> "But the scientists have discovered something else – a kind of miracle that could save us. If we can protect 50% of our planet from human exploitation, our ecosystem will be able to stabilise and regenerate. Life on Earth will recover!
>
> "Our governments have already promised to protect a quarter of the planet, so we know it's possible. But no other global movement is championing this miracle recovery plan! The Avaaz organization is trying to raise money for the next critical 25%.
>
> "It's up to us.
>
> "If 50,000 of us chip in just the cost of a cup of coffee a week, we can make the proposal famous, face down the polluters and poachers, and campaign to get leaders to drive through a deal to save the planet at the Global Summit on Biodiversity."

I understand that the Summit scheduled for September 2020 has been postponed. So there is still time to make your influence felt.

The other exception is as follows:

"Of all the things that have happened in recent years none has given me renewed hope as much as the reaction of American students in the aftermath of mass shootings. 'We are the students, we are the victims, and we are the change, fight gun violence now! Student organizers wrote for one of the planned events.

"On a number of occasions American students have demonstrated that they are much more mature and better qualified to govern than the politicians who not only tolerate, but protect the right of the public to buy and use automatic rifles. Wouldn't it be wonderful if these students could elect a Congress that would make possession illegal, compensate owners for surrendering these lethal weapons, and then literally melt them down and use the metal to make hand tools for the poor people of the world. An exercise of common sense of that magnitude would restore hope everywhere."[8]

I mention this in appreciation of the students who marched, and also as a lead back to the miracle of George Floyd. His brutal and inhumane death has ignited a power beyond imagination. Rich people, poor people, black people, white people, Aboriginal people, straight people and gay people have joined forces in a true demonstration of the Creator's universal love for all creation. Their staying power indicates the kind of political power that can move mountains.

Until now the Cabal has been able to buy politicians with generous campaign donations and biased support from the press it controls. The temptation will persist. But when the peoples' army of hope and light form ranks on the political battlefield the light can and will prevail.

I would be less than honest if I didn't remind readers of Marine Captain Randy "Captain Kay" Cramer's warning that there would be an attack on Earth from 18 to 24 months from September 2019. "If what I say starts to happen just when you think it can't be any crazier, I want people not to be shocked."[9]

Capt. Cramer, who served at a U.S. base on Mars for 17 years, didn't say who would be attacking whom. Would it be the Nazis from U.S. bases on Mars? [10] Or would it be the Nazis and their Reptilian allies from bases in Antarctica, and elsewhere on Earth. But it doesn't need to happen. If the people's political army persuade the United States Congress to defund the U.S. Nazi-controlled military, the odds of an attack actually happening will be greatly reduced. Military expenditures should be defunded by 50% at once. That is the exact amount they were increased following the Khazarian Israeli false flag attack on the New York Trade Center on September 11, 2001. But it has to be directed reduction that includes the Space Force and other sensitive areas that I have mentioned.

In the event that an attack should take place we still have reason to be optimistic. I am informed that space ships from several planets that belong to the Galactic Federation of Light are already stationed at the ready to come to our rescue. The members of the Federation are all very spiritual and totally loyal to the one they call The Source, The Forever, The One, that we refer to as the Creator God. They are on our side.

They also have plans to assist us Earthlings to a higher dimension which most of our Extraterrestrial cousins already enjoy. Not only will we be able to walk on water, and go through what we know as solid walls, at some stage we will be able to materialize or dematerialize at will. To achieve this higher dimension, however, we will have to become much more spiritual and substitute love, the glue that binds the Cosmos together, for hate. So, the future is amazingly bright although our rite of passage may be a little bit rocky.

If you are interested in a post-grad course in what I call "The Broader Reality," please read a good cross-section of the books listed in the Bibliography.

NOTES

DISCLOSURE NOTES:

1. Col. Philip J. Corso, *The Day After Roswell*, (New York: Pocket Books, 1997.)

2. Len Kasten, *The Secret History of Extraterrestrials: Advanced Technology and the Coming New Race*, (Rochester: Bear & Company, 2010).

3. Telephone conversation with Clifford Stone June 2018.

4. The Bible, Exodus, Chapters 7-12.

5. Memorandum E-A10, 19 October 1940, Council on Foreign Relations, War-Peace Studies, Baldwin Papers, Box 117.

6. Len Kasten, *The Secret History of Extraterrestrials: Advanced Technology and the Coming New Race*, (Rochester: Bear & Company, 2010), p. 5

7. Len Kasten, *Alien World Order: The Reptilian Plan to Divide and Conquer the Human Race*, (Rochester: Bear & Company, 2017), p. 260.

8. *Ibid.*

9. As passed on to me by Carol Rosin personally.

10. "Rebuilding America's Defenses: Strategy, Forces and Resources for a New Century. A Report of the Project for the New American Century, September 2000."

11. "NATO / OTAN." *What Is NATO?*, www.nato.int/nato-welcome/index.html.

12. Senator Daniel K. Inouye at the Intra-Contra public hearings 1987.

13. Steven M. Greer, *Hidden Truth, Forbidden Knowledge: Its time for you to know.* (Crozet: Crossing Point, Inc. 2006).

14. Dr. Michael Wolf, former NSA consultant in an interview with Chris Stoner, October 2000.

15. John Loftus, America's Nazi Secret, Trine Day, November 2010.

16. David Rockefeller, *Memoirs*, (New York: Random House, 2002), p. 405.

17. James Hansen, *Storms of My Grandchildren: The Truth About the Coming Climate Catastrophe and Our Last Chance to Save Humanity*, (New York: Bloomsbury USA, 2009).

18. Stoner, Chris. "Dr. Michael Wolf." *Life of Dr.Michael Wolf*, Oct. 2000, galactic.no/rune/micwolf3.html

19. Dr. Russell Blaylock, What Chemtrails Are Doing To Your Brain – Neurosurgeon Reveals Shocking Facts: https://youtube.com/watch?feature=player_embedded&v=X31W-TGG1k0

20. Dane Wigington, *Geoengineering: A Chronicle of Indictment, Exposing The Global Climate Engineering Cover-Up.*

21. Gordon Duff, *Documentary Proof: University of North Carolina Genetics COVID-19*, 18 April, 2020.

22. Flynn, Jerry, *Hidden Dangers – 5G*, JFG Publishing, p.223.

23. *Ibid.*

24. Dafna Tachover, https://childrenshealthdefense.org/news/chds-dafna-tachover-talks-about-5g-dangers-with-rt-america/, January 2020.

25. Sheetz, Michael. "FCC Approves SpaceX to Deploy up to 1 Million Small Antennas for Starlink Internet Network." *CNBC*, CNBC, 20 Mar. 2020.

CHAPTER 1: A LITTLE HISTORY OF MONEY

1. Holy Bible, The New King James Version. Thomas Nelson Inc., 1983, Genesis 47, Verses 13-17, p. 48.

2. Francis T. Lui, "Cagan's Hypothesis and the First Nationwide Inflation of Paper Money in World History," Journal of Political Economy, Vol. 91, #6, 1983, pp. 1067-74, in *Major Inflations in History*, Forrest H. Capie (ed.). Aldershot: Edward Elgar Publishing Limited, 1991, pp. 210-212.

3. *Ibid.*

4. William Chaffers, *Gilda Aurifabrorum: A History of English Goldsmiths and Plateworkers, and Their Marks Stamped on Plates*. Reeves & Turner, [1800], p. 210.

5. *Ibid.*

6. William F. Hixson, *Triumph of the Bankers: Money and Banking in the Eighteenth and Nineteenth Centuries*. Westport: Praeger Publishers, 1993, p. 46.

7. *Ibid.*, p. 60.

8. Ellis T. Powell, *The Evolution of the Money Market – 1385-1915*. New York: Augustus M. Kelley, 1966, p. 197.

9. *Ibid.*, pp. 117-118.

10. *Ibid.*, p. 129.

11. Mary Quayle Innis, *An Economic History of Canada.* Toronto: The Ryerson Press, 1935, p. 28.

12. Richard A. Lester, "Currency Issues to Overcome Depressions in Pennsylvania, 1723 and 1729." *The Journal of Political Economy*, Vol. 46, June 1938, p. 216.

13. Larry Elliott Economics (Editor) *The Guardian*, "Richest 62 people as wealthy as half of the world's population, says Oxfam," January 18, 2016.

14. Prince Charles while attending the Davos Conference, 2020.

CHAPTER 2: ENGLISH COLONISTS WERE MONETARY PIONEERS

1. Lester, Richard A., "Currency Issues to Overcome Depressions in Pennsylvania, 1723 and 1729", *The Journal of Political Economy*, Vol. 46, June 1938, p. 326.

2. Hixson, William F., *Triumph of the Bankers*, op. cit., p. 46.

3. Lester, Richard A., "Currency Issues to Overcome Depressions in Pennsylvania, 1723 and 1729", op. cit., p. 338.

4. *Ibid.*, p. 341.

5. Smith, Adam, *Wealth of Nations*, New York: P.F. Collier and Son, 1909, p. 266.

6. Nettles, Curtis P., *The Money Supply of the American Colonies before 1720*, op. cit., p. 265.

7. Ferguson, E. James, *The Power of the Purse: A History of American Public Finance, 1776-1790*, Chapel Hill: University of North Carolina Press, 1961, p.16.

8. Hixson, William F., *Triumph of the Bankers*, op. cit., p.81.

9. Franklin, Benjamin, *The Writings of Benjamin Franklin*, Albert Henry Smyth (ed.), New York: Macmillan, 1907, (9), pp. 231-233.

10. Mitchell, Broadus, *The Price of Independence*, New York: Oxford University Press, 1974, pp. 401-403.

11. Hixson, William F., *Triumph of the Bankers*, op. cit., p. 80.

12. *Ibid.*

13. Morris, Richard B., *The Forging of the Union 1781-1789*, New York: Harper & Row, 1987, p. 155.

14. Hixson, William F., *Triumph of the Bankers*, op. cit., p. 115.

15. Sumner, William Graham, *A History of American Currency*, New York: Augustus M. Kelley, 1968, p. 123.

16. Gouge, William M., *A Short History of Paper Money and Banking in the United States*, New York: Augustus M. Kelley, Part II, 1968, p. 45.

17. Angell, Norman, *The Story of Money*, New York: Frederick A. Stokes Co., 1929, p. 294.

18. Hixson, William F., *Triumph of the Bankers*, op. cit., p. 150.

19. Bordo, Michael D., "Gold Standard", in *Encyclopedia of Economics*, David R. Henderson (ed.), New York: Warner Books, Inc., 1993, p. 359.

20. *Ibid.*

21. For budget discussions see U.K. Parliamentary Debates, Vol. clxxxiii, col. 55.

22. *Ibid.*

23. Bordo, Michael D., "Gold Standard", op. cit., p. 360.

CHAPTER 3: THE BUBBLE ECONOMY

1. Hon. Paul Hellyer In a Keynote Address to the International UFO Congress, Fort McDowell Resort, Scottsdale, Arizona, Saturday, February 26, 2011.

2. Quill, Greg, "Rogers hike will make rate country's highest", in *The Toronto Star*, Wednesday, July 13, 1994, p. D6.

3. *The State of the World's Children*, 1992, *Summary*, New York: Oxford University Press, pp. 8-11.

4. *Ibid.*

5. Isabel V Sawhill, in essay *"Poverty in the United States"* for the *Encyclopaedia of Economics*.

6. President's Council of Economic Advisers in 1981 report.

7. *Funny Money*, Paul T. Hellyer, p. 130

8. *Ibid*, p.131.

9. *Ibid*, p.131.

CHAPTER 4: A PLETHORA OF IDEAS

1. *The Fortune Encyclopedia of Economics*, p. 836.

2. *Ibid.*

3. Korten, David C. *When Corporations Rule the World. Berrett-Koehler Publications, Inc., 2015.*

4. *The Pecora Investigation,* The Senate Committee on Banking and Currency, March 4, 1932.

5. Ferdinand, Lundberg, *America's 60 Families* (New York: Vanguard Press, 1937), p. 102-3.

6. *The Trouble with Billionaires*, Linda McQuiag & Neil Brooks, Penguin Canada, p. 47.

7. Friedman, Milton, "A Monetary and Fiscal Framework for Economic Stability", in *American Economic Review*, XXXVIII, June 1948.

8. Friedman, Milton, *A Program for Monetary Stability*, New York: Fordham University Press, 1959, p. 65.

9. *Ibid.* Henry C. Simons, "A Positive Program for Laissez Faire: Some Proposals for a Liberal Economic Policy," in his *Economic Policy for A Free Society* (Chicago, 1948), pp. 65-5 (first published as "Public Policy Pamphlet, No. 15, ed. Harry D. Gideonse (Chicago, 1934); Lloyd W. Mints, *Monetary Policy for a Competitive Society* (New York, 1950), pp. 186-87. Albert G. Hart, "The 'Chicago Plan' of Banking Reform,' *Review of Economic Studies*, 2 (1935), pp. 104-16. Reprinted in Friedrich A. Lutz and Lloyd W. Mints (eds.), *Readings in Monetary Theory* (New York, 1951), pp. 437-56.

10. Fisher, Irving, *100% Money*, New York: The Adelphi Company, 1935.

11. Hixson, William F., *Triumph of the Bankers: Money and Banking in the Eighteenth and Nineteenth Centuries*, Westport: Praeger Publishers, 1993, p.49.

12. Nicolay, John G., and Hay, John (eds.) *Abraham Lincoln: Complete Works*, New York: The Century Co., 1907, 2: p. 264.

13. Hixson, William F., *Triumph of the Bankers*, op. cit., p. 134.

14. Hammond, Bray, *Sovereignty and an Empty Purse*, Princeton: Princeton University Press, 1970, p. 192.

15. Campbell, Alexander, *The True Greenback*, Chicago: Republican Books, 1868, p.31.

16. McCulloch, Hugh, *Men and Measures of Half a Century*, New York: Charles Scribner's Sons, 1888, p. 201.

17. Myers, Margaret G., *A Financial History of the United States*, New York: Columbia University Press, 1970, p. 198.

18. McPherson, Edward (ed.), *A Hand-Book of Politics*, New York: Da Capo Publishing Corp., 1972, p.271.

19. Blackmore, John H., *Hansard*, Vol. 6, 3rd Session, July 24, 1956, p. 6368.

20. Confirmed in telephone conversation with Robert Thompson on July 7, 1994.

21. Simons, Henry C., *Economic Policy for a Free Society*, Chicago: University of Chicago Press, 1948, pp. 65-66.

22. Information provided by Professor John H. Hotson, Executive Director. The Committee of Monetary and Economic Reform, August 8, 1994.

23. *"Michael" Journal*, Quebec: July-August, 1994, p. 17.

24. Fisher, Irving, *100% Money*, New York: The Adelphi Company, 1935, p. 20.

25. Friedman, Milton, *A Program for Monetary Stability*, op. cit., pp. 65-66

26. *Ibid*, p. 18.

CHAPTER 5: THE LONG, LONG ROAD TO DISCOVERY

1. Friedman, Milton, in a footnote reply to a letter from William F. Hixson, November 9, 1983.

2. Friedman, Milton, in a letter to Professor John H. Hotson, February 3, 1986.

3. *Ibid.*

4. Gerald K. Bouey, speech to the 46th Annual Meeting of the Chamber of Commerce, Saskatoon, September 22, 1975.

5. Hellyer, Paul. The Money Mafia: a World in Crisis. Trine Day LLC, 2016.

CHAPTER 6: BANK FOR INTERNATIONAL SETTLEMENTS

1. Adam Lebor, *Tower of Basel,* (New York: Public Affairs, 2013), p. 197.

2. http://www.treaties.un.org/Pages/showDetails.aspx?objid=0800000280167c31

3. http://www.bis.org/about/index.htm?1=2

4. BIS History: http://bis.org/about/history.htm

5. Adam Lebor, *Tower of Basel,* op. cit., p. xviii.

6. Harold Callender, "The Iron-Willed Pilot of Nazi Finance, *New York Times,* March 4, 1934.

7. Adam Lebor, *Tower of Basel,* op. cit., p. xix.

8. See R. Billstein, *Working for the Enemy: Ford, General Motors and Forced Labor in Germany During the Second World War,* (New York: Berghahn Books, 2000). In the late 1990s Ford opened its archives and commissioned archivists and historians to scrutinize its wartime record. Their findings are compiled in a 208-page report, published in 2001. "Research Findings About Ford-Werke Under the Nazi Regime," is available at http://media.ford.com/article_display.cfm?article_id=10379. The report also notes that Ford and its subsidiaries in Allied countries made a crucial contribution to the Allied war effort, producing vast amounts of aircraft, military vehicles, engines, generators, tanks, and military ordinance.

9. Adam Lebor, *Tower of Basel,* op. cit., p. 106.

10. Henry Morgenthau diaries, Book 755, Bretton Woods, July 16-18, 1944, pp. 9, 21.

11. *Ibid.*

12. John Easton, Economic Warfare Division, to Secretary of State, London, November 27, 1944. NARA. Author's [Adam Lebor] collection.

13. Adam Lebor, *Tower of Basel,* op. cit., pp. 156-157.

14. Dulles Cable, March 27, 1945, NARA. RG22, Entry 134, Box 162.

15. Morgenthau diaries, FDRML. Book 755, Reel 216, p. 183.

16. Allen Dulles to Joseph Dodge, September 20, 1945. NARA. OMGUS-FINAD. RG260, Box 237. File: Johannes Tuengeler. The extracts from the bankers' biographies are taken from this document. The author [Adam Lebor] is grateful to Christopher Simpson for generously supplying copies of this document, which he unearthed in the U.S. National Archives.

17. *Ibid.*

18. Neal H. Petersen (ed.), *From Hitler's Doorstep: The Wartime Intelligence Reports of Allen Dulles 1942-1945,* (Penn State University Press, 1996), pp. 426-427.

19. *Ibid.,* p. 628.

20. Adam Lebor, *Tower of Basel,* op. cit., p. 187.

CHAPTER 7: MONETARISM IS MACHIAVELLIAN

1. Carroll Quigley, *Tragedy and Hope: A History of the World in Our Time,* (Angriff Press, 1975).

2. Friedman, Milton, in a footnote reply to a letter from William F. Hixson, November 9, 1983.

3. *Annual Report of the Council of Economic Advisers,* Washington, D.C., January 1981, p. 34.

4. Source: Q.&W. – OECD National Accounts; P=CPI in IMF Financial Statistics Yearbook. Labour Force – OECD Labour Force Statistics.

5. Friedman, Milton, and Friedman, Rose D., *Free to Choose: A Personal Statement*, New York: Avon Books, 1981, p.11.

6. Weintraub, Sidney, *Capitalism's Inflation and Unemployment Crisis: Beyond Monetarism and Keynesiasm*, New York: Addison-Wesley Publishing Company, Inc., 1978, p.104.

7. Friedman, Milton, and Friedman, Rose D., *Free to Choose: A Personal Statement*, op. cit., p. 251.

8. Excerpt from an article by Stephen Labaton, "10 Wall St. Firms Settle with U.S. in Analyst Inquiry," *New York Times*, April 29, 2003.

9. Excerpt from an article by Brian Miller, "There's little repentance on Wall Street these days," *Globe and Mail*, April 28, 2003.

10. David Henry and David Ingram, "Settlement talks heat up at JP Morgan," *Globe and Mail*, September 27, 2013.

11. Bill Black, "Documents in JP Morgan settlement reveal how every large bank in U.S. has committed mortgage fraud," TheRealNews.com, November 29, 2013.

12. Tanya Talaga, "Swiss bankers helped hide billions from U.S. taxes, senators say," *Toronto Star*, February 27, 2014.

13. Nicholas Shaxson, *Treasure Islands: Uncovering the Damage of Offshore Banking and Tax Havens*, (New York: Palgrave Macmillan, 2011).

14. Ellen Brown, "The Leveraged Buyout of America," *Web of Debt Blog*, August 26, 2013.

15. Ellen Brown, "The Global Banking Game Is Rigged, and the FDIC Is Suing," *Web of Debt Blog*, April 13, 2014.

CHAPTER 8: THE CORONAVIRUS CATASTROPHE

1. Wall Howard, Phoebe. "Hairstylist and Doctors Played Key Role in Design of Ford Face Shield." Toronto Star, 1 Apr. 2020, p. B1.

2. McKinley, Steve. "Chilling Timeline Finally Lifts Veil on Nova Scotia Massacre, as Province Moves from Hell toward Healing." *Toronto Star*, 24 Apr. 2020, p. 12.

3. Kevin Bissett and Adina Bresge, The Canadian Press as reported in the Toronto Star Sunday, April 26, 2020.

4. The Canadian Press

5. *Ibid.*

CHAPTER 9: THE BIGGEST HEIST IN HISTORY

1. G. Edward Griffin, *The Creature from Jekyll Island: A Second Look at the Federal Reserve*, (Westlake Village: American Media, 2002), p. 24.

2. Jack Metcalf, *The Two Hundred Year Debate: Who Shall Issue the Nation's Money*, (Olympia: An Honest Money for America Publication, 1986), p. 91.

3. *Ibid.*, p. 92.

4. "J.P. Morgan Interests Buy 25 of America's Leading Newspapers and Insert Editors." U.S. Congressional Record, February 9, 1917, p. 2947.

5. Milton Friedman and Anna Jacobson Schwartz, *A Monetary History of the United States 1867-1960*, (Princeton: Princeton University Press, 1963).

6. *Ibid.*, pp. 327-328.

7. Josey Wales, "First Audit Results In The Federal Reserve's Nearly 100 Year History Were Posted Today, They are Startling!" *Before It's News*, September 1, 2012.

8. Ellen Brown, *Was the Fed Just Nationalized? Did Congress just nationalize the Fed? No. But the door to that result had just been cracked open.* Published by Common Dreams on Friday, April 03, 2020.

9. *Ibid.*

CHAPTER 10: THE KAZARIAN CONNECTION

1. Preston James, PhD. Social Psychologist.

2. Wikipedia

3. Ibid.

4. Ibid.

5. Information provided to me personally by the pastor of the church when my wife and I drove him from Yorkminster Baptist Church, Toronto, to the Royal York Hotel.

6. Len Kasten's, Dark Fleet, p. 137.

7. Ibid.

8. Len Kasten, Dark Fleet: The Secret Nazi Space Program and the Battle for the Solar System.

9. Richard Boylan, PhD., one of the longest serving and most knowledgeable ufologists anywhere.

10. Len Kasten, Dark Fleet, p. 184.

11. Forbidden Knowledge TV.

CHAPTER 11: THE SOLUTIONS

1. Greer, Steven M., and Steve Alten. Unacknowledged: an exposé of the World's Greatest Secret. A & M Publishing, L.L.C., 2017.

2. Alien Cosmic Expo

3. Weiner, Tim. *Legacy of Ashes: the History of the CIA*. Penguin, 2011.

4. Joyce Nelson Nelson, Joyce. *Beyond Banksters: Resisting the New Feudalism*. Watershed Sentinel Books, 2016.

5. *Ibid.*

6. Zuesse, Eric. "Why Post-Coronavirus America Will Have Massive Poverty." *Modern Diplomacy*, 23 Apr. 2020, moderndiplomacy.eu/2020/04/24/why-post-coronavirus-america-will-have-massive-poverty/.

7. Valone, Thomas. *Zero Point Energy: the Fuel of the Future*. Integrity Research Institute, 2009.

8. Dr. Wolf (Kruvante) Stonor, Chris. "Dr. Michael Wolf." *Life of Dr.Michael Wolf (Kruvante)*, Oct. 2000, galactic.no/rune/micwolf3.html.

CHAPTER 12: CLEANING UP THE SWAMP

1. Estulin, Daniel. *TransEvolution: the Coming Age of Human Deconstruction*. Trine Day, 2014.

2. Don Schmidt and Thomas J. Carey, *Witness to Roswell: Unmasking the 60-year cover-up*, (Franklin Lakes: New Page Books, 2007), p. 39.

3. The Money Mafia: a World in Crisis, by Paul Hellyer, Trine Day LLC, 2016, pp. 248–249.

4. WikiLeaks Reveals US Military Use of IMF, World Bank as "Unconstitutional Weapons" by Whitney Webb, February 7, 2019.

5. As reported in the Toronto Globe & Mail, May 6, 1998.

6. As reported in the Wall Street Journal, October 13, 1998.

7. *Ibid.*

8. Mark Landler, "Scandal Hinders I.M.F's Role in Global Lending," New York Times, October 22, 2008.

9. Kevin Carmichael, "Mideast Called on to Shore up IMF," Globe & Mail, November 3, 2008.

10. Les Whittington, "No G20 cash for euro rescue," Toronto Star, November 5, 2011.

11. Joseph E. Stiglitz, *Globalization and its Discontents*, (New York: W.W. Norton & Company, Inc., 2002), pp.106-107.

12. The Money Mafia: a World in Crisis, by Paul Hellyer, Trine Day LLC, 2016, pp. 261–262.

13. Dr. Hans Blix, Weapons of Mass Destruction Commission, "Weapons of Terror," June 1, 2006, p.94.

14. Moore, Mike. "Robert 'Bobby' Kennedy Jr. Joins the Podcast and Drops Absolute Bombshells on Bill Gates, Dr. Fauci, the CDC, FDA, Govt. Vaccine Kickbacks and the List Goes On in a Raucous EXCLUSIVE Sit Down." 2020, podcasts.apple.com/us/podcast/ep-18-robert-bobby-kennedy-jr-joins-podcast-drops-absolute/id1491435111?i=1000471537466. Accessed 2020.

15. From a translated text of Osama bin Laden's broadcast taken from the New York Times, October 8, 2001.

CHAPTER 13: LET THE LIGHT SHINE IN

1. Mark Siljander in a private telephone conversation.

2. Lincoln, Abraham. "The Emancipation Proclamation." National Archives and Records Administration, National Archives and Records Administration, 2000, www.archives.gov/exhibits/featured-documents/emancipation-proclamation.

3. The Bible, Genesis, vs. 1-31.

4. Google

5. Z. Zhu, et. al. *Hominin occupation of the Chinese Loess Plateau since about 2.1 million years ago,* https://www.nature.com/articles/s41586-018-0299-4.epdf?

6. See the National Aeronautics and Space Administration sketch in the pictures section.

7. *Ibid.*

8. *Hope Restored: My Life and Views on Canada, the U.S., the World & the Universe*, by Paul Hellyer, Trine Day LLC, 2018, pp. 236..

9. Randy Kramer, speaking at the Alien Cosmic Expo, Toronto, September 22, 2019.

10. *Dark Fleet: the Secret Nazi Space Program and the Battle for the Solar System*, by Len Kasten, Bear & Company, 2020, pp. 120–120.

BIBLIOGRAPHY

Birkenfeld, Bradley C. *Lucifer's Banker: the Untold Story of How I Destroyed Swiss Bank Secrecy*. Greenleaf Book Group Press, 2016.

Boylan, Richard J. *Star Kids: the Emerging Cosmic Generation*. Blue Star Productions, 2005.

Brown, Courtney. *Cosmic Voyage: a Scientific Discovery of Extraterrestrials Visiting Earth*. Hodder & Stoughton, 1997.

Cameron, Grant. *Contact Modalities: The Keys to the Universe*. Its all connected Publishing, 2020.

Corso, Philip J., and William J. Birnes. *The Day After Roswell*. Simon & Schuster Inc., 2017.

Dolan, Richard M. *UFOS and the National Security State: Chronology of a Cover-up 1941-1973*. Hampton Roads Pub. Co., 2002.

Estulin, Daniel. *True Story of the Bilderberg Group*. Trine Day, 2017.

Freeland, Elana. *Chemtrails, HAARP, and the Full Spectrum Dominance of Planet Earth*. Feral House, 2014.

Freeland, Elana. *Under an Ionized Sky: from Chemtrails to Space Fence Lockdown*. Feral House, 2018.

Flynn, Jerry G. *5G Hidden Dangers: How governments, telecom and electric power utilities suppress the truth about the known hazards of electro-magnetic field (EMF) radiation*. JGF Publishing, 2020.

Good, Timothy. *EARTH: an Alien Enterprise*. THISTLE Publishing, 2014.

Greer, Steven M., and Steve Alten. *Unacknowledged: an exposé of the World's Greatest Secret*. A & M Publishing, L.L.C., 2017.

Griffin, G. Edward. *The Creature from Jekyll Island: a Second Look at the Federal Reserve*. American Media, 2010.

Hansen, James, and Makiko Sato. *Storms of My Grandchildren the Truth about the Coming Climate Catastrophe and Our Last Chance to Save Humanity*. Bloomsbury, 2011.

Harris, Paola Leopizzi. *UFOs: All of the Above and Beyond*. CreateSpace 2016.

Hellyer, Paul. *A Miracle in Waiting: Economics That Make Sense*. Authorhouse, 2010.

Hellyer, Paul. *Light at the End of the Tunnel: a Survival Plan for the Human Species*. AuthorHouse, 2010.

Hellyer, Paul. *The Money Mafia: a World in Crisis.* Trine Day LLC, 2016.

Howe, Linda Moulton. *Glimpses of Other Realities: Volume II: High Strangeness.* LMH, 2018.

Kasten, Len. *The Secret History of Extraterrestrials: Advanced Technology and the Coming New Race.* Bear & Co., 2010.

Kasten, Len. *Secret Journey to Planet Serpo: a True Story of Interplanetary Travel.* Bear & Company, 2013.

Lanza, R. P., and Bob Berman. *Beyond Biocentrism: Rethinking Time, Space, Consciousness, and the Illusion of Death.* BenBella Books, 2017.

Loftus, John. *America's Nazi Secret: an Insider's History of How the United States Department of Justice Obstructed Congress by: Blocking Congressional Investigations into Famous American Families Who Funded Hitler, Stalin and Arab Terrorists; Lying to Congress, the GAO and the CIA, The.* TrineDay, 2010.

McQuaig, Linda, and Neil Brooks. *The Trouble with Billionaires.* Langara College, 2019.

Nelson, Joyce. *Beyond Banksters: Resisting the New Feudalism.* Watershed Sentinel Books, 2016.

Perkins, John. *Confessions of an Economic Hitman.* Berret-Koehler Publishers, 2004.

Siljander, Mark D. *Deadly Misunderstanding: Quest to Bridge the Muslim/Christian Divide.* Bridges To Common Ground, 2016.

Sparks, Jim. *The Keepers: an Alien Message for the Human Race.* Wild Flower Press, 2008.

Stiglitz, Joseph E. *Globalization and Its Discontents.* Penguin Books, 2017.

Styles, Chris, and Graham Simms. *Impact to Contact: the Shag Harbour Incident.* Arcadia House Publishing, 2013.

Weiner, Tim. *Legacy of Ashes: the History of the CIA.* Penguin, 2011.

Wood, Judy D. *Where Did the Towers Go?: Evidence of Directed Free-Energy Technology on 9/11.* New Investigation, 2010.

Wood, Ryan S. *Majic Eyes Only Earth's Encounters with Extraterrestrial Technology,* (Bloomfield: Wood Enterprises, 2005).

ABOUT THE AUTHOR

Paul Hellyer is Canada's Senior Privy Councillor, having been appointed to the cabinet of Prime Minister Louis S. St. Laurent in 1957, just eight years after his first election to the House of Commons in 1949 at the age of 25. He subsequently held senior posts in the governments of Lester B. Pearson and Pierre E. Trudeau, who defeated him for the Liberal Party leadership in 1968. The following year, after achieving the rank of senior minister, which was later designated Deputy Prime Minister, Hellyer resigned from the Trudeau cabinet on a question of principle related to housing.

Although Hellyer is best known for the unification of the Canadian Armed Forces, and for his 1968 chairmanship of the Task Force on Housing and Urban Development, he has maintained a life-long interest in macroeconomics. Through the years, as a journalist and political commentator, he has continued to fight for economic reforms and has written several books on the subject.

A man of many interests, Hellyer's ideas are not classroom abstractions. He was born and raised on a farm and his business experience includes manufacturing, retailing, construction, land development, tourism and publishing. He has also been active in community affairs including the arts, and studied voice at the Royal Conservatory of Music in Toronto. His multi-faceted career, in addition to a near-lifetime in politics, gives Hellyer a rare perspective on what has gone wrong in the critical fields of both world politics and economics.

In recent years he has become interested in the extraterrestrial presence and their superior technology that we have been emulating. In September 2005 he became the first person of cabinet rank in the G8 group of countries to state unequivocally "UFO's are as real as the airplanes flying overhead." He continues to take an interest in these areas and provides a bit of basic information about them in this book.

By 2012 Hellyer was convinced that the New World Order announced by President George H. Bush was just a screen for a 70 year old plan by the Nazi Party to establish a Fourth Reich in cooperation with their Reptilian Allies.

Their plan for World domination included depopulation on a massive scale. So Hellyer is recommending immediate action to prevent the catastrophe from occurring.

PHOTOGRAPHS

Defence Minister Hellyer in his role as President and Chancellor of the Royal Military College, Kingston, Ontario, conferring the degree of Honourary Doctor of Law on his first political boss, the Right Honourable Louis S. Laurent, Prime Minister of Canada, 1948-1957, at Fall Convocation, October 3, 1964.

Dr. Edgar Mitchell, Apollo 14 astronaut, arrives at the Hellyer residence for dinner, July 7, 2006, accompanied by his friend, Susan Swing and Susan Boyne (later Bird) wife of Mike Bird who took the picture.

The Hellyers at lunch with international journalist Paola Harris, and Dr. Courtney Brown, Director of The Farsight Institute, at the Society for Exploration Conference, Boulder, Colorado, June 2008.

The Hellyer family celebrating Paul's 90th birthday, August 6, 2013.

Paul coming in for a landing at Arundel Lodge, Muskoka, Ontario.

Defence Minister Hellyer with his deputy-minister, chairman of the Defence Research Board, the chiefs of staff, and Associate Minister Lucien Cardin after a meeting with General Lyman Lemnitzer, Commander in Chief of Allied Forces in Europe

Paul and his bride Sandra on their wedding day October 1st 2005

Paul with Sandra Hellyer and Kay Hotaling in Lebanon, on a tour of the Middle East.

Paul dropping in to say hello to President Gerald Ford at a formal dinner in Toronto.

Paul presenting a copy of his book *Light at the End of the Tunnel: A Survival Plan for the Human Species*, and a bottle of good Canadian ice wine to President Jimmy Carter at a reception in Plains Georgia.

187

Chemtrails originating from Billy Bishop Airport being released directly over the world famous Toronto Sick Children's Hospital

If you look up and see the chemtrails in the sky you will become aware of a dangerous practice.

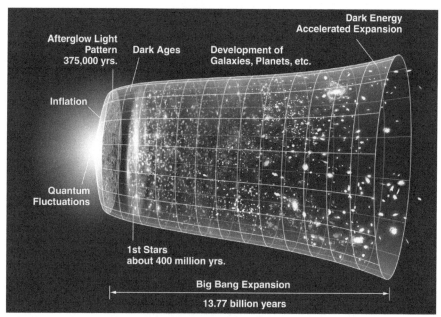

A sketch of the Big Bang

Valiant Thor, the Benevolent Venutian Alien with an I.Q. of 1200, who offered Earthlings a better, richer, healthier life in exchange for giving up our nuclear weapons. His offer was not accepted.

Index